Managing Your Business Risk in the Cybersecurity Minefield

Critical Strategies from
21 Cybersecurity Experts

Prominence Publishing

www.prominencepublishing.com

Managing Your Business Risk in the Cybersecurity Minefield -- 1st ed.

ISBN: 978-1-988925-84-4

Contents

Foreword

By Chris Wiser

As a business owner, one of the biggest concerns I have is protecting what I consider the greatest assets to my company: our employees, our business assets, and our confidential data. If I cannot protect these extremely important assets from malicious intent, I am not doing my job as a business owner. Many business owners I have spoken to understand what cybersecurity is but fail to understand the WHY behind the NEED for cybersecurity.

I am sure by now you have heard the saying, "It is not IF you are hacked but WHEN." If you have heard that in the past and have thought it was not true – it is time to start opening your eyes to the impact that cybercrime is having on our business community. We have seen an increase in cyberattacks in the news across the world, and there is no safe place that business owners can go to avoid cybercrime. It is a fact of business and at this point, every business owner needs to implement some form of cybersecurity plan to help protect their greatest assets from being stolen.

Cybercrime affects all businesses, whether large or small, no matter where they're located or who is involved. As technology advances and we continue to live in a digital world, it is crucial to understand that Cybersecurity should be the number one concern for all business owners. Business owners that are not protecting their employees or safeguarding their assets and confidential data are at great risk.

If you have been turning your head the other way when it comes to cybersecurity, it is crucial to understand that NO BUSINESS is too small or too large to avoid this, and you need to start preparing for the worst-case scenario. At the very least, your business should hire a cybersecurity expert, implement a strong cybersecurity plan and take necessary steps to protect your business from cybercrime. If you are a business owner, the time is NOW to start caring about your business and take Cybersecurity seriously!

Chris Wiser,

CEO, 7 Figure MSP

Speaker/Trainer/
Entrepreneur Coach

Why and How to Outsource Your Cybersecurity

By Amir Sachs

The Money Tree

Before really sinking into this book, take a moment to sit comfortably in your chair, relax, and imagine you have a "Money Tree". Yes, yes, a real Money Tree. One you could go to every day and pick money off of its branches, in whatever currency you would like.

This magical tree would produce money as long as you treat it well. To get money from this tree, you would need to water it, expose it to just the right amount of sunlight, and clean the weeds around it. However, you live in an open neighborhood with a lot of foot traffic — strangers can look into your garden and see your beautiful Money Tree. Perhaps they could even steal money from the tree or steal the tree altogether.

Would you do anything that it takes to protect your tree?

Of course you would — you might put a tall fence around it, install sophisticated alarm systems, or hire professional armed security guards. Hell, I would do a DNA sequencing on the tree to make sure it can be regrown just in case something terrible happens to it.

"But Amir, we live in a reality where there are no Money Trees," I hear you say.

Well, I have good news for you: your business is your Money Tree!

Running a business today means you need computer systems to communicate and interact with the outside world. Even if you are a manual manufacturing plant with no automation at all in your manufacturing process, you still need to email vendors and clients, and keep track of your stock levels, orders, and invoicing. Every business nowadays needs computers to operate.

A successful business needs to get value for money from absolutely everything involved. One of the first and most vital areas to consider is your IT infrastructure, specifically, your IT support partner.

The first lockdown in 2020 showed a lot of businesses that their IT support partners were not partners at all.

When it came to the crunch, these IT support companies were just another supplier, with no real commitment to their clients. We have heard from many companies who experienced their IT support disappearing in March of 2020, and in subsequent lockdowns afterwards.

Just when they most needed IT support and expertise, BANG, their IT support vanished into thin air. Their IT vendor was simply too busy, or too unprepared for such an event.

In the rush to transition to working from home, business owners took shortcuts, exposing their computer networks and suffering security breaches and ransomware. The worst happened: their Money Tree stopped growing money.

Over the past few years, we have witnessed a huge rise in something called ransomware. You will read a lot about ransomware throughout this book. But for now, know that you absolutely want to avoid it.

If you use any technology in your business – whether it's something as simple as a cash register, or it's a full-blown network for five locations – a proper IT strategy will be your best friend. It's the foundation for growing your business. It can mean the difference between surviving a time of uncertainty and thriving through it.

I have written this chapter to help you understand how a trusted IT support partner behave and what great IT support looks like. You will learn how good cyber security partners genuinely partner with their clients and refuse to become just another supplier. I'll also explain why it's critical that you put your IT strategy and data security at the very core of your long-term business planning.

Let's start.

Don't Get Confused By Tech Talk

A good cyber security partner will not confuse you with terminology you do not understand. They will talk business with you, not tech.

When choosing a new cyber security partner, conduct an initial conversation with them and see how you feel at the end of it. Are you confused? Did you understand everything you were told? If not, try finding someone else. Companies like this might be great technologists, but they do not understand business principles and so will let you down when you will need them the most.

As illustrated by the Money Tree story at the beginning of this chapter, I love analogies! I use them daily when talking to people in order to bridge the gap between technology and business. Find a partner who can speak your language, one that will not make you feel dumb when you're conversing. A true professional!

Experience

A true cyber security partner can show examples of their work in the field. They will be able to provide you with contactable references for existing and past clients. They will be able to clearly demonstrate how they help their clients.

Ask them questions like:

- How do you go about implementing backup systems?
- How often are you performing backup restoration to make sure we have everything you need in case of a disaster?
- Do you have any whitepapers detailing how your technology has "saved the day"?

Again, ask yourself, did their response make sense to you? Did you understand everything they said?

I will let you in on a little secret. When I interview new vendors, I often ask questions that I already know the answer to, just to see if the vendor has any idea what he's talking about. It's a true "bullshit detector."

I recommend you ask the questions in such a way that you will be able to determine whether the response is real or just "sales talk."

Custom Solutions

While most cyber security firms like to provide package services which are easily deployed, the top partners will customize a solution to your exact, unique needs. One size does not fit all in cyber security as it is a risk-based environment. When talking to a potential partner, make sure they show interest in your business and have tried to understand how you operate. If the conversation is sales-y and very little interest is shown in your business, run.

Instead, look for a partner who has a genuine interest in trying to understand how you do things in your business and can show experience in similar environments. These will be the kind of partners who won't disappear in hard times.

Trust

Do your research. Trust is not something which is easily discovered initially when you don't know the person you are talking to. A few easy checks can help you here. Look up the person you are talking with on LinkedIn as well as the CEO of the company. Do they write a blog? Have they published any whitepapers or books? If you get to talk to their existing clients, ask the question "Do you trust ..." and follow up with "Why do you trust?"

You want to work with people who have experience in the type of environment you operate. Ask questions about their experience and how long they have been doing cyber security. Listen to the answers carefully and see if you can trust them or not.

You know you're talking to the right cyber security partner when you ask them, "Using all the technologies you suggest, will I get ransomware?" and the answer is, "I can't guarantee you won't, but if you do, we can get you back up and running within a reasonable amount of time."

If after the first discussion you get a feeling that you're not sure about the company, don't engage. There are plenty of good and trusted cyber security companies around.

Cover All Your Bases

Progress in technology waits for no one.

Now, more than ever, there are many potential entry points if one wants to break into your business. Tomorrow, there will be more. Your new IT support partner should be able to protect you from all current and future threats, provided they keep up with advancements in technology.

As a non-tech person, you might not be able to distinguish between old/outdated technology and new technology, but you can ask questions about how your potential IT company up with the times. Ask them questions like:

- How often do you evaluate the effectiveness of your solutions?
- How did you deal with the last hack/breach/ransomware attack?
- How do you protect us from hacking/phishing/ransomware?

Are the answers full of tech jargon or are they business-like and explained in a way you understand? You don't want confusing tech jargon thrown at you as it can be confusing. If you don't understand the answers, ask them to explain them in a different way.

Training, Procedures and Policies

Of all successful hacks, 95% are a result of human error. What training is your proposed IT partner suggesting you take and is that training included in their fee?

You will need training, procedures, and policies on:

- Phishing and social engineering
- Business email compromise
- Password management
- Data responsibility
- Unauthorized software and internet use

Strengthening the weakest link is the cornerstone of cyber security. This should be an ongoing process and not a one-off event. Training should include both self-learning modules as well as an interactive, regular training session where users can ask questions and get real live answers.

Why Outsource?

In my daily dealings with potential clients, I often hear, “I have an internal IT team, I don’t need to outsource this to a third party.” If you have an internal IT person/team, well done for covering this important side of your business.

The questions you want to ask yourself are:

- Is this the best ROI I can get for my budget?
- What happens if my main IT person leaves? Who will be able to take over from there?

- Do I have full documentation of everything that's being done on a regular basis?
- Is the latest technology being used in my business?
- Is there a password safe that you have access to which contains all the usernames and passwords to manage your business?

I know I'm biased. I own Blue Light IT, which is a successful cyber security company and I want you to outsource your needs to us. But we get calls on a regular basis from companies whose internal IT person was either fired or left, and now they can't access various vital resources in their business. It's like having your Money Tree cared for by a full-time gardener, only to find out the gardener is gone, he has moved the tree, and didn't tell you where he moved it to.

When outsourcing cyber security to a reputable cyber security company, you are assured that your business is protected by professionals who: always update their skillset with the latest technologies and train your staff regularly. This is so that you'll have all the backups and assurances that even in the case of a successful attack on your business, you will be able to recover and return back to business as usual within your specified timeframe.

With the right cyber security partner, you can sleep well at night knowing your Money Tree is looked after and cared for.

About the Author

Amir Sachs is an information technology executive with 25+ years of experience in the SME market across multiple industry sectors. He is appointed as a trusted vCIO and CTO for multiple companies, both in the US and internationally.

In 2003, Amir founded Blue Light IT, based out of Boca Raton, Florida, where he and his team provide cyber security services, IT management, and strategic technology direction for companies of all sizes.

Prior to founding Blue Light IT, Amir owned and managed various businesses in the manufacturing, distribution, retail, hospitality, and import/export. The experience gained in these businesses gives Amir the ability to quickly understand the myriad of challenges his clients experience and enables his firm to provide technology-based solutions.

Amir's favorite quote is, "Impossible, it's only a level of difficulty."

Amir is available for speaking engagements and consulting.

Contact Amir on:
LinkedIn: www.linkedin.com/in/amirsachs
Facebook: fb.com/mspbocaraton

Avoiding Cyber Security Risk

By Brian Artigas

It was the Wednesday morning before Thanksgiving weekend. Mary, the office manager at a local medical practice, was going through her email as quickly as possible. She came across a message from Tina, her friend from a supplier for the office. Mary was expecting a secure document from Tina and she was sure this was the document she was waiting for. Tina's message included a link to view the document. Mary clicked the link, and it took her to a very official looking Microsoft SharePoint page with a link to the filename in the middle of the page. She clicked the link, and it took her to a Microsoft 365 sign-in page prompting her to enter her email credentials to view the document. She signed in without even thinking about it, but nothing happened. Mary thought, That's odd, but you know how computers are.

Mary had a lot of work to get through before the end of the day so she sent an email to Tina stating that she could not open the message and carried on. Finally, at 5:00pm, she set up her email vacation message notifying people that she would be out of town for a week and left for paradise.

Unfortunately, Mary had been scammed. She entered her email credentials into a hacker's fake SharePoint page.

Her credentials were now part of the hacking organization's database and within two short hours, the hackers had downloaded the contents of Mary's mailbox including her calendar and contacts. The hacker learned that Mary was on vacation and would be gone for a week. Over the weekend, the hacker mined Mary's mailbox and extracted every email address from every person with whom she had ever corresponded. Then the hacker repurposed the same message and sent the same attack to the mined email addresses. Several of Mary's co-workers and friends fell for the scam and then the real damage started. Mary's mailbox had personal information: medical details on hundreds of patients. It would only be a matter of time before the hackers leveraged those records in another attack or sold them on the dark web. Mary has now become a "business email compromise scam" statistic.

The above story is true, though the names and some of the details have been changed. In this case, since Mary's organization is a medical practice based in

Florida, her company is subject to HIPAA regulation and the Florida Information Protection Act. This breach is likely going to cost their insurance company upwards of $1 million in fines, remediation costs, lost profits, and lost trust from the practice's patients.

Just think, this whole ordeal could have been avoided if Mary recognized that phishing email and did not open it. I know this story well because we had just met with Mary a few weeks earlier to talk about improving their cyber security posture but they hadn't made a decision to engage us yet. We received one of the emails sent by the scammer from Mary's mailbox. While one of our engineers investigated the email to determine its severity, I reached out to notify Mary's office of the attack and we were authorized to begin executing our incident response procedures. After all of this occurred, my company was contracted to secure her organization's network and manage their cyber security going forward.

Mary is not the only one to experience this type of attack. According to the 2020 Internet Crime Report by the FBI's Internet Crime Complaint Center, this attack happened to 241,342 victims in 2020 alone to the tune of over $54 million in damages. What's worse is that from this type of attack, hackers can carry out various other attacks and scams posing as the person to whom the compromised account belongs. That same report states that business email compromise scams were responsible for over $1.8 billion in damages in 2020.

How do you avoid Mary's situation? How do you protect yourself and your business?

Risk Analysis

The first step in avoiding and controlling cyber security risk is to identify the risks posed to your organization by performing a risk analysis. If you don't know where your leaks are, you have no chance of plugging them.

Data Discovery

The first step to risk analysis is determining what kind of data your organization holds and where it lives. If you're a medical office, your data is ePHI (electronic protected health information) and it typically lives in your EMR/EHR (electronic medical records/electronic health records) software. If you're an accountant or attorney, your data is PII (personally identifiable information) which is any information that directly identifies an individual such as a name, address, social security number, or other identifying number or code, telephone number, email address, etc. For some attorneys, your data could also be ePHI depending on what type of law you practice. That data could live in your business's industry-specific applications and/or it can also live on your workstations, server, cloud storage, and email.

Almost every business contains some form of protected information. If your organization runs payroll, you have PII in the form of employees' social security numbers, names, addresses, etc. If you run credit cards, you may have credit card numbers stored in your systems. If you're a property manager for an apartment complex or homeowners' association, you might run credit checks for tenants or prospective buyers.

Keeping Your Data

Many of my clients ask me if they should just get rid of sensitive data. They ask something to the effect of, "Do I need to get rid of all of this data?" The answer is no, you just need to protect it. In most cases, you need the data to support your business. Using a house analogy, you don't throw away the valuables in your house because someone could steal them; you protect them by locking your doors and windows, setting your alarm, or living in a gated community.

Threat Discovery

Once you have determined where all your data lives and document those locations, it'll be easier to identify and document the potential threats and vulnerabilities to the Confidentiality, Integrity and Availability (CIA) of that data. Here are some examples of threats to consider:

- Physical theft of computers, servers, flash drives, or other storage devices
- Exfiltration due to a non-existent or improperly configured firewall

- Exfiltration from a malware-infected phone being charged by a workstation's USB port
- Exfiltration from a compromised Internet of Things (IoT) device on the organization's main network
- Malware such as keyloggers, trojan horses, or remote access tools
- Ransomware
- Flood or fire
- Data loss due to power outages
- Disgruntled or untrained employees.

Security Measure Assessment

Consider all of the security measures you currently have in place. These include administrative, physical, and technical measures such as:

- Policies and Procedures
- Employee cyber security awareness training
- Door locks
- Antimalware software
- Data backups

Now that you have a list of known threats and what you have already put in place to protect your data, you can start to work on ways of handling the remaining threats.

For each threat, you'll want to determine how you're going to manage it. You ultimately have four options:

- **Avoid** – Avoiding risk means not engaging in any function or activity that would expose you to a risk.
- **Control** – Whatever risk you cannot avoid, you try to control. Controlling risk is putting measures in place to minimize your risk exposure. This can be administrative controls such as business disaster recovery plans, it can be physical such as door locks, or it can be technical such as antimalware software or backing up your data regularly.
- **Acceptance** – Accepting a risk means doing nothing to avoid or mitigate the risk. If the cost to mitigate the risk is much higher than the cost the risk could incur, one may choose to just accept the risk.
- **Transfer** – Transferring risk is somehow transferring risk ownership from yourself to someone else. This is often done through contracts and insurance policies.

The final steps in cyber security risk analysis are determining the cost each threat could present to your organization versus how much the security measure will cost to implement. If the cost of security measures significantly outweighs the cost of a risk negative outcome, you may decide to accept the risk or even transfer it to an insurance company.

It's worth mentioning that there are cases where you cannot transfer or accept the risk. If you're a regulated organization, you may be legally required to address or control the risk. You also may not be able to transfer it; your insurance company may not cover a claim if you do not have certain security measures in place. Which brings me to another point: read the fine print on your cyber liability insurance policy.

Avoiding Cyber Security Risk

Multi-Factor Authentication

One of the best controls you can put into place to avoid risk is enabling multi-factor (MFA) or two-factor authentication (2FA) for as many applications and systems as possible. For 2FA, the person signing in with their username and password is also required to produce a code that usually changes every 30 seconds. In most cases, this code is provided by a mobile application such as Duo, Microsoft Authenticator, or Google Authenticator, but some sites and services may offer less secure methods such as sending you a text message, email, or call you with the code. Some password managers can provide the 2FA code in place of a mobile device. If an attacker manages to steal your password and they don't have the 2FA code, they will not be able to access your account.

Employee Cyber Security Awareness Training

It's very difficult to avoid a cyber security risk if you don't know what it looks like. By providing your employees with an effective cyber security awareness training program, they learn what the risks look like so they can avoid them.

Remember that the training must be effective. Be wary of training programs out there that simply satisfy a regulatory requirement. An organization gathers its employees into a large room, they all sign a piece of paper to prove they attended, and a speaker lectures for an hour on the subject at hand. The signed paper goes into a regulatory evidence book and in the business thinks they've satisfied the regulatory requirement. No test is provided to confirm that employees have retained the information. I have witnessed people sitting in these classes scrolling through social media, texting, even sleeping. I think it's a safe bet that those folks probably didn't retain much of the material. It only takes one employee falling for a simple phishing email to bring an organization to its knees or give an attacker access to your company's network.

Documented Policies and Procedures

Just as you would provide an employee with a job description to communicate expectations, they also need cyber safety rules to abide by. When I hire a new employee, the first few days of their employment is orientation. After they fill out the government-required paperwork, they start their cyber security awareness training and take their test. Then they log into a portal where they read and agree to our policies and procedures.

The following is not an exhaustive list, but almost every business should, at a minimum, have the following policies:

- Acceptable Use Policy: This policy dictates how an employee may use company-owned electronic devices such as desktop computers, notebooks, tablets, and cell phones.
- Password Policy: This policy states the required complexity of a password as well as how and where the password is stored. This policy should also mandate multi-factor authentication wherever supported.
- Employee Sanction for Non-Compliance Policy: If an employee doesn't adhere to your documented policies and procedures, this policy dictates how your organization will handle the situation.
- Incident Response Plan: In the event of a breach, it's important to have a process to deal with it. Who is the incident reported to, how is the incident investigated and how do you resolve the incident? The worst time to try to answer these questions is while an incident is occurring.

Email Protection Service

Another way to avoid risk is to employ an email protection service to reduce spam and phishing attacks. If the phishing emails are eliminated before your employees see them, then you've avoided a pretty significant risk. It's important to note that this does not replace a good cyber security awareness training program. Many of the phishing and spam filters on the market do a very good job, but none of them are 100% effective.

Password Management

In addition to your password policy, you can use an enterprise password manager to significantly reduce the chances of a compromise due to a stolen password. With a password manager, you can enforce the complexity portion of your password policy; some will handle the two-factor authentication as well. One nice feature of many password managers is that they have a plug-in you can install in your browser. When you open a webpage, the plugin will present you with the option to log in for you, so you don't have to worry about typing or copying and pasting your credentials. This presents an excellent benefit for avoiding malicious links. To someone in a hurry or not paying attention, the web address offlce.com or öffïċë.com may look a lot like office.com, but your password manager's plugin will be able to tell the difference and will not offer up credentials to log into that site.

UTM Firewall

A unified threat management (UTM) firewall uses multiple systems to both avoid and control risk on your network. One system used to avoid risk is web content filtering, which monitors what web addresses, devices, or people are visiting and prevents them from visiting malicious sites. The packet filtering feature of the firewall blocks access to all incoming traffic that was not requested unless a rule has been created to allow it. This prevents a hacker from attacking susceptible applications on your network that should not be made public such as Microsoft Terminal Services (AKA Remote Desktop), and Telnet. UTM firewalls also have an intrusion detection and prevention system (IDS/IPS) that watches all the traffic coming in and going out of your network to detect malicious activity. A properly configured firewall will be able to detect specific attacks such as brute forcing and consequently block the offending IP addresses. Most UTM firewalls have many other features such as anti-malware, network access control, DNS filtering, and virtual private network (VPN) services. An entire chapter could be written on UTM firewalls. Suffice it to say, it's important to have a UTM firewall with a currently supported security subscription.

Conclusion

This chapter is certainly not an exhaustive list of things related to cyber risk avoidance but I hope I've provided you with some useful and actionable information you can use towards identifying and avoiding risks on your network. I also hope I've opened your eyes a bit to how one small mistake by one employee can create an absolute nightmare scenario for an entire organization. One small error can not only affect a business' employees and owners, but also, like in the case of Mary and the medical office, all of the patients of an organization.

About the Author

Brian Artigas began tinkering with computers as a child living in Vero Beach, Florida in the 1980s. His love for computers and technology landed him his first job building and repairing computers at a small local computer store in 1997.

In 2001, he started a web hosting company called Netrodyne Interactive Communications while working as a lead technician for a small IT company in Tequesta, FL called Allstate Sales & Leasing. In 2003, he was offered the opportunity to acquire the IT company. He purchased the assets of Allstate Sales & Leasing, combined them with Netrodyne's, and founded Allstate Computers.

Today, Allstate Computers is a managed IT services provider located in Jupiter, FL. Allstate specializes in providing security-first IT solutions, network management and cloud services. Their clients range from three to over 300 employees. Brian and his team have developed a proven IT, cyber security compliance, and risk management program designed to eliminate the burden on businesses owners of managing and securing IT systems themselves. Allstate's mission is to partner with its clients to transform IT systems from a necessary evil into a tool for success.

You can reach Brian online at:

https://www.linkedin.com/in/brianartigas

For some tools to help you assess your risk and to learn more about managing it, visit:

https://www.allstatecomputers.com/managing-your-business-risk-book

Allstate Computers

(561) 743-1521 / (855) IT-GURUS

www.allstatecomputers.com

Why Employees are the First Line of Defense

By Matthew Bora Kaing

First Security Breach

Our office received an alarming after-hours call from a manufacturing firm, desperate and in panic mode. The company was very concerned about emails being sent from their finance director to one of their customers asking for a change in payment method to a new bank account. The emails were also asking for a stop on all pending checks and redirection to the new bank account. However, although these emails were coming from the finance director's email account, they were not sent by their finance director!

Wanting to help in quick order, we met with their CEO and in-house IT person to get a better understanding of the situation and to figure out what happened. The manufacturing firm asked us to perform a security assessment and provide recommendations on how to avoid this issue in the future. During this process, we discovered that the finance director's email account was compromised by a hacker that sent emails to the company's customers regarding open and current invoices. This was a planned, strategic attack in the email communication thread which deliberately timed and sent the crafted email regarding payment. Clearly, the hacker had been watching the communication for the right time to strike! The customer was notified of what happened and that the new bank account information was a fraud from a hacker.

We spent the next several days analyzing the manufacturing company's email system to track who and from where the compromised account was accessed. We interviewed the accounting staff, IT staff, and checked the email system logs. We found that the compromised account was being accessed using web mail from multiple locations (from different states and outside the US).

As we continued to discuss the details with the designated IT person, we learned that this was the SECOND time their email was compromised (that they know of), and the CEO wanted us to help prevent this from happening again.

Second Security Breach

In a second case, the IT director of a large construction firm contacted us about an email issue with their CEO.

Emails were being sent out to all employees and customers on behalf of the CEO using Outlook Contacts. This was all done without the CEO's knowledge! The email subject line was, "Please review and sign your company Accounting Invoice 84XXX via DocuSign." The company's IT director asked us to work with his in-house IT team and perform a security review to determine the cause of the compromise and then make recommendations for going forward.

These types of scenarios are not uncommon. In fact, 92.4% of cyber attacks are delivered via email.[1] "Human error is one of the biggest weaknesses exploited by cybercriminals, and 17% of the tactics they utilize come in the form of social attacks."

In both the scenarios mentioned, the hacker (via email account) was impersonating the finance director and CEO. The hacker used their email accounts to send out messages to customers asking them to pay invoices or transfer money.

Both the finance director and CEO did not have any malicious intent when clicking on the email that allowed the compromise to happen, but they were the unknowing "gateway" that enabled the hacker into the company network. With the right amount of social engineering, exploiting these individuals' good nature, they were tricked into clicking on a link in an email that allowed the hacker to gain access to the corporate email systems and send personal messages

---

[1] https://enterprise.verizon.com/en-gb/resources/reports/dbir/2018/

to all contacts. As a result of these incidents, the business' reputation is damaged and the business loses money because of the downtime needed to investigate and report the incident to law enforcement. To prevent future incidents like this, all users (the CEO, finance director, and employees) must be part of the solution. All staff need to understand the importance of cyber security, how they can help protect the company data, and that they need to report any security issues right away.

The Impact of COVID

Cyber attacks are way up since people started working from home in 2020. According to IBM, the average time to identify and contain a breach in 2020 was 280 days. The average total cost of a data breach was $3.86 million.[2] People working from home often have fewer security defenses on their home network than they would have in the office. For example, many people use a wireless network at home that is not protected or have a home network without any firewall. Some employees who use home computers for company business also do not have the latest antivirus or the most recent security updates (for both the operating system and software applications).

We would like to share a few ways to help protect you and your company from a cyber attack:

---

[2] https://www.ibm.com/security/data-breach

1. Security Training and Policies – Provide training for all your employees and contractors about data security, email attacks, and your company's policies and procedures. Employees need to understand how important cyber security is to your company and your bottom line. They need to know how they can protect against phishing scams, phone scams, and how to report a security incident.
2. Encrypt Sensitive Files – Most likely, your computer and company server have sensitive data stored or saved on them. You would want to encrypt specific data or files, yet still allow the designated company personnel access to the information. Each employee could encrypt their entire disk drive using Windows 10 BitLocker and MacOS. However, it would be better to encrypt only the files and folders where the sensitive data is stored. This requires specialize software that your IT professional can help with.
3. Encrypt Sensitive Email Messages – If you send email messages that contain sensitive information like social security number, credit card, and personally identifiable information (PII), encrypt the email. Companies can set up secure email in Office 365, Google Workplace (G-Suite), and use a third-party solution like ZixMail.
4. Controlled Access/Least Privilege Policy - Your company most likely has sensitive

information and customer data. Restrict access to only the individuals that need the data to perform their job. Segment the data into different job roles or departments and give access only to employees or contractors that must have access. For example, set up different network share and security permissions for the finance, engineering, and operations departments. Don't give your CEO, president, or office manager full administrator permission to the server or email systems; to manage risk, set up a separate service account if one is required. Have policies and procedures to remove access after an employee is terminated.

5. Anti-Virus - Have anti-virus and anti-malware installed and running in a pro-active mode on your computer with daily updates and scans. Use the latest next-gen antivirus advanced endpoint detection and response software.
6. Strong Password with Multi-Factor Authentication – Use strong passwords that have 12 characters or more, along with multi-factor authentication for email, applications, and network access. This security feature verifies "it is you" trying to access an account. Set up two-step authentication for your Office 365 or Google G- Mail when you log on to access email or on-line storage such as OneDrive or G-Drive. Two-step authentication is what online banking

systems use – you must enter a username, password and one-time code or text message code to complete the log on process.

a. For Office 365, here is the step-by-step Setup Instruction Guide for two-step verification:

https://support.office.com/en-us/article/set-up-2-step-verification-for-office-365-ace1d096-61e5-449b-a875-58eb3d74de14

b. For Google Apps or Google Workspace, here is the step-by-step Setup Instruction Guide for two-Step verification:

https://support.google.com/a/answer/9176657?hl=en

7. Use a Password Manager – This helps you create a strong password and saves you time. In today's busy world, we have so many passwords to remember for various accounts, it is almost impossible to keep track of all of them. It is recommended that you use a professional password manager to help you create a strong and unique password for each account. For example, we have setup Last Pass, Keeper Security, and RoboForm for many of our customers. Using your browser's password manager is okay for individual home use, but it does not provide

full management, security, and reporting compared to third- party business password manager.

8. Be Careful When Using Public WiFi for Conducting Your Business - Using public WiFi or hotspots at Starbucks or hotels can be a very risky activity. This is because you do not control the wireless device or the internet you are going through. Hackers can be monitoring the wireless connection and capturing the information.

You should consider the following safeguards when using Public WiFi:

- Use a VPN, SSL Connection and turn off sharing on your computer if you must use public WiFi.
- Use the company's latest VPN client version for SonicWALL SSL VPN or Global VPN, Fortinet, and Cisco VPN client to connect to your office.
- When using a web browser, confirm you are using the security protocol SSL connection. For example, in a Chrome web browser, it will have an SSL lock pad icon on display in the URL bar (see snapshot on the next page).

  https://support.google.com/a/answer/9176657?hl=en

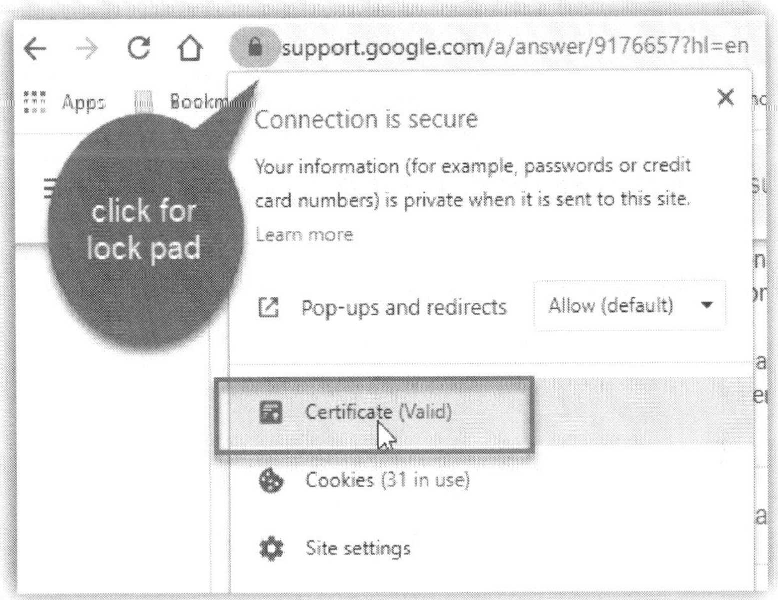

9. Update Software and Security Patch Promptly – Promptly update Windows 10 or MacOS and applications to protect against known vulnerabilities. Use only the vendor-supported release of your application software. For example, do not use old versions of Windows 7, Microsoft Office, Antivirus or QuickBooks that are no longer supported or are out-of-warranty by the software vendors. They will not have the latest security updates/patches available anymore and hackers are looking for ways to exploit these weaknesses.

10. Online Web Meeting Tools – Many people are using online web conferences to host video conferences, chat, and text message one another. It is very important to be aware of the ways these tools might impact your digital privacy and security. Free products from Zoom, Skype, Google Meet, and Slack might collect and store your information and retain messages. Read the vendor privacy rules to understand how they track users and what is stored. You should consider using your company web meeting tools so you can control your own privacy. If you have Office 365, Google G- suite, or Zoom, configure corporate-wide security policies such as requiring meeting passwords, waiting room, or sharing of information.
11. Backup and Check Your Data – Back up your files, email, and online applications, but test the backup regularly (monthly or quarterly). Your data and customer information are the most valuable things to you and your company. It is important to automate the process of backing up your data to the cloud and to also save a backup data copied locally for easy recovery. You should also have data-loss prevention policies to protect sensitive information from getting sent outside your company or uploaded to online storage. If you do not have a good solution for backing up your workstation, you can use OneDrive for Business, Google Drive Sync, and

Windows backup to save a copy to an external drive. Test the backup to ensure it works!

Conclusion

Network security is not a one-time event. Do not "set it and forget it." With a more mobile workforce, anywhere-access to company email and applications, employees are being targeted with phishing email or through social media. Thus, educating your employees about cyber security, along with on-going monitoring of your network security is critical to preventing a data breach. You want to avoid your company's reputation from being tarnished in the news or in any other way.

If you would like to learn how we can help, including managed cyber security and proactive IT services, and employee security awareness training, download our free audiobook, "Avoid these Five Deadly Computer Disasters and Save Your Business." Click on Free Stuff at www.eSudo.com or schedule a complimentary strategy consultation by calling us at 408-216-5800.

About the Author

Matthew Bora Kaing wants to make a positive difference in the lives of people by what he does! He is the president of eSudo Technology Solutions, Inc. in San Jose, CA (Silicon Valley). He has a strong desire to help people use technology. With an engineering degree and after working for large IT companies, like IBM and Cisco Systems, Matthew and his friends started an IT consulting firm that focuses on serving small businesses. For the last 20 years Matthew built and train his team to help small businesses to improve performance, operate, and manage risk leveraging modern technologies.

Many business owners spend most of their hours running their company, serving customers, and using technology to automate operations. Businesses of every size and industry are increasingly dependent on technology. For all of the benefits that technology brings, it also creates risk at a magnitude never previously imagined. Who can help the small business owners learn and manage the ever increasing changes of technology? Most IT vendors do not take the time to understand or are unable to help the businesses manage their risk. It is essential to know your company's risk, address the vulnerabilities, and Matthew understands how to protect what you have built today and tomorrow because "you don't know what you don't know".

eSudo specialize in helping law firms, insurance brokers, and construction companies grow more clients through essential technologies and improve productivity without risking security. eSudo deploys a pro-active solution that works and increases productivity by effectively managing risks.

Call 408-216-5800 or https://www.eSudo.com for a COMPLIMENTARY consultation to learn the eSudo difference can make to help your business thrive. Secure your business peace of mind!

Mitigating Today's Cyber Risks for Your Business

By Brian Galli

It's April 2020. Your entire staff is doing their best working remotely from home. You've finally figured out how to get everyone connected and working again — servers, VPNs, Slack, stand-up desks, etc. Smoother sailing at last, then BAM! Your entire network is held for ransom. William clicked on a link in an email that appeared to be from you, the CEO, asking him to quickly order Postmates gift cards for the team to treat them for all their hard work. "So kind!" William thinks, as he clicks immediately to make the gesture happen. Now what?

Since COVID-19, the US FBI reported a 300% increase in reported cybercrimes.[3] It's highly likely that you've either experienced a situation like this or know someone who's had to deal with one, whether a small business, global corporation, or personal instance.

There's good news and bad news when it comes to today's cyber threat reality.

The bad news is that every business, large and small, has more cyber-threat-related risks to manage than ever before and no company in the world can be 100% protected. Cyber attacks have skyrocketed since spring of 2020 and there's no sign of that slowing down. Hackers are getting more and more creative in capitalizing on universal uncertainty, remote work security holes, and employees who lack awareness of the latest hacking tactics. Spam, malware, ransomware, phishing, vishing, smishing — it seems like every day you hear a new rhyme about a way to get hacked.

What's at stake? At minimum, disruption in productivity, and, at worst, companies may experience financial and reputation losses that can be business-ending. In 2020, 43% of cybersecurity breach victims were small and medium businesses,[4] and the average cost of a breach for those businesses is $200,000,[5]

---

[3] "15 Alarming Cyber Security Facts and Stats." Cybint, 12 Jan. 2021, www.cybintsolutions.com/cyber-security-facts-stats

[4] "2020 Data Breach Investigations Report." Verizon Enterprise, 2020, enterprise.verizon.com/en-gb/resources/reports/dbir

[5] Hiscox Group, 2019, Hiscox Cyber Readiness Report 2019, www.hiscox.com/documents/2019-Hiscox-Cyber-Readiness-Report.pdf

causing 60% of small businesses that were attacked to go under within six months of the incident.[6]

Now for the good news! The good news is that there are proactive practices that any business can take right now to mitigate cyber threat risks, no matter the size of their business.

You might be thinking, "Keeping up with IT was tough enough. Add in managing cyber risk and my head is spinning!" You're right. It's a lot! For most small and mid-sized businesses, keeping pace with the ever-evolving world of IT and making the right strategic decisions to power a business is mission-critical, but often a huge challenge. It makes sense to outsource the management to an external team of professionals whose job it is to not only manage an IT network and provide robust support, but also help mitigate cyber risk for you.

Xperts Unlimited, the managed IT department (MID) of small and mid-sized businesses in Los Angeles and Orange County, has been doing just that for more than 20 years. Seasoned professionals when it comes to building and maintaining bespoke technology foundations for growing businesses, Team Xperts is on a mission to educate businesses about keeping their businesses productive and protected.

---

[6] Freeze, Di. "60 Percent of Small Companies Close Within 6 Months of Being Hacked." Cybercrime Magazine, 16 Oct. 2019, cybersecurityventures.com/60-percent-of-small-companies-close-within-6-months-of-being-hacked

So where do we start? The following approach will help you get a pulse on your own company's unique risk and provide guidance on how to operationalize a plan to mitigate that risk. Keep in mind, the goal is mitigation of risk and building a culture and technology foundation of awareness, preparedness, and resiliency. It's not a matter of if you'll get hacked, but when, and how severe the outcome.

With so much cyber risk out there and no way to be 100% protected, you may ask, why bother? The best analogy is to think of it like the security measures you'd use for your own home — from the perimeter to each of the rooms: fences, security cameras, dead bolts, motion sensors, etc. And don't forget about the valuables you have inside that need protection. If someone really wanted into your house, they could do it, but the layers of protection you've created will certainly minimize the damage, or hopefully deter an intruder all together.

Back to protecting your business! To outline the steps in mitigating cyber risk for your business, we'll use the tried-and-true change management framework of People, Process, and Technology.

Step 1: People — Create Awareness and a Human Firewall

Employees are a company's biggest asset, but also the biggest source of risk. The best technology in the world can't stop an employee from being socially engineered. Ninety-five percent of cybersecurity breaches are due to human error1. Making cyber security awareness and vigilance part of your company culture is critical and should be championed from the top.

Xperts Unlimited Recommends:

A. Leadership making cyber security a priority and talking about it often across the organization. This transparency will keep security top-of-mind for employees.

B. Adopting a cyber security training program that not only has annual training, but ongoing training and testing (ideally on a weekly basis).

C. Implementing a simulated phishing email program to test employees monthly.

Step 2: Process – Plan for Resilience

As mentioned earlier, no company on the planet can be 100% hack-proof. It's a matter of when, not if, a hack will be attempted on your business. However, more than 77% of organizations do not have a Cyber Security Incident Response Plan,1 hence why 60% of small businesses end up going out of business when hacked. We recommend devising a robust Cyber Security Incident Response Plan that accounts for disasters and cyber attacks, and making sure the following are in place and reviewed often.

Xperts Unlimited Recommends:

A. An employee handbook that includes policies like: Acceptable Computer Use, Bring Your Own Device (BYOD) Protocols, Breach Incident Reporting & Procedures, etc.

B. Learn your state laws on data privacy and breach remediation requirements.

C. Get a cyber liability insurance policy.

D. Schedule quarterly Strategic Business Risk Reviews with your managed IT department (MID) or managed service provider (MSP) to review your risk on an ongoing basis and understand how you might need to pivot to shore up protections over time.

E. Understand where risk lives within your network and data, identify employee vulnerabilities, and if your company's information is being sold on the dark web.

Step 3: Technology – Leverage the Right Tools to Mitigate Risk

From issuing patches on a schedule to leveraging the latest tools for maintaining good cyber hygiene, technology is your best friend when it comes to cybersecurity risk mitigation. We recommend partnering with a seasoned managed IT department (MID) that can help you get a sense of your true risk. They can then implement, manage, and evolve the right tools for your unique business and risk profile.

Xperts Unlimited Recommends:

A. Managing – A solid IT network foundation will leverage several key tools that act like a home's security system. These tools include antivirus, firewalls, anti-ransomware, anti-phishing, email encryption, password managers, and the list goes on. MIDs can keep your network up-to-date and select the right mix of security tools needed for your level of risk based on the assessment done on your network, data, employees, and dark web presence. Engaging an MID can mean a small investment in protection versus losing your business completely.

B. Monitoring – No single human could possibly keep an eye on every moving part of a business's IT network. Nor should they. MIDs and their experts will leverage monitoring tools, like SIEM (Security Information and Event Management), SOC (Security Operations Center), and NOC (Network Operations Center) to provide alerts, many of which now use AI to tune in to patterns of events that may otherwise go undetected for weeks or months.

C. Evolving – It is important that you stay up on news and trends in cyber security but lean on an MID to be your expert guide on the rapidly-changing tech and risk landscape. Partner with an MID that puts as much focus on security as they do on productivity and allows you to not sacrifice security for convenience. They will make recommendations during Quarterly Business Risk Reviews that will help your business stay protected over time.

That was a lot! The takeaways? Our global threat landscape has changed drastically — cyber attacks are on the rise and here to stay. While no business can be risk-free, closing the risk gap is very doable. Small and midsized businesses need to be proactive, rather than reactive, and follow the above steps to protect what they've built, minimize disruption, and avoid financial and reputation loss. Ultimately, you will need to find a trusted technology partner (a managed IT department with a focus on cyber security) that has invested in the tools, technology, and expertise needed to execute these steps comprehensively and continuously.

People, process, and technology. Xperts Unlimited helps businesses effectively mitigate their unique exposure around these three key aspects. We'd love to meet you to learn more about your business and how we can help do the same for you.

Please visit us at www.xpertsunlimited.com to request a complimentary consultation for your business.

About the Author

Brian Galli,
Commander-in-Chief of
Xperts Unlimited

After witnessing so many businesses frustrated with slow tech support, unpredictable pricing, and a break-fix mentality, Brian Galli set out to do IT better for businesses in Los Angeles and Orange County. Brian wanted his own MSP (Managed Service Provider) to be seen as a true strategic growth partner; dedicated to keeping IT simple and fair, while being the powerhouse foundation of any growing business.

Twenty years later, Brian and the Xperts Unlimited team have become the go-to solution for small and mid-sized companies looking to have the best-managed IT and cybersecurity in town. An LA native, Brian loves giving back to the community and helping fellow business neighbors thrive. He's always had a passion for technology and continually evolving Xperts Unlimited's services with the times, inspiring his team and clients to do the same.

Brian's vision for Xperts Unlimited is to help businesses become the most productive and protected in the US by harnessing the ever-more-paramount world of IT.

With 50+ clients throughout the area, having helped businesses grow from three to 300 people, and being integral members of their clients' teams (some for almost two decades), Brian and Team Xperts Unlimited are proud to be the leading IT & Cybersecurity Services Partner in LA and OC.

When Brian's not being Team Xperts' Commander-in-Chief, he enjoys having fun with his soulmate and three children, Kenpo Karate, and anything tech related!

Interested in partnering with Brian and Xperts Unlimited? Get in touch at www.xpertsunlimited.com.

Cybersecurity 101

By Felipe Isaza

There are few times if ever I yell, "Rip the cable out of the modem!" But early in the morning one day after a big scare, I was on the cusp of giving that very command. Its everyone's worst nightmare. Being cyber attacked ranks way up on the list of things you hope will never happen. But sadly, it does. Not on our watch as IT providers, mind you — well at least we make it very difficult for hackers with all the layers of security we implement. Cyber security is a prevalent reality you must be vigilant about.

My nervous, now new client, was practically in full panic mode. I had to strain hard to even decipher what he meant in his current state. "I am logged into my server," he told me, "however not able to open Sage, Print, nor open any of my files."

Luckily, I was able to remotely log into his system and within minutes calm him down. His screen was jittery and practically strobing out on him. In addition to his justifiable fear of being cyber attacked and his data wiped out, this was not something that instilled confidence to the untrained eye. That type of flickering would drive most of us to go all "Office Space" on our very own electronics.

I realized his system had been compromised and the "threat actor" was still logged on. This is what we call a robbery-in-progress, so my first reaction was the aforementioned — ripping off any cables right from the wall. As dramatic and cinematic that might have looked, there are other ways to begin damage control and establish a beachhead against any more theft. Despite a thorough check-up, I realized the culprit had encrypted the entire system and was now holding its contents ransom. A message by the hacker led to a Bitcoin ransom note to the tune of $4500. With some communication back and forth, along with a payment sent in the form of cryptocurrency, we successfully recovered the files.

This is just one scenario of a breach that would not have happened had this company gone with us in the first place. We would have instituted what we here at FUNCSHUN call "a zero-trust framework" and in this case, security really begins with not trusting anybody, as sad as that may sound. Studies show about 30% of organizations were unsuccessful in acquiring their data back following a ransomware payment. So, in order not to get to that point, we suggest you keep all avenues into your system as watertight as possible. We excel in this on many levels.

Cyber Security and Your Business

How much time did you spend online today? How many hours were you working, scrolling, posting, liking, interacting, sending invoices? With the internet being a pillar of business and life today, one of the most important pieces is often overlooked: cyber security.

If you spent any amount of time online today, you were putting yourself and/or business at risk. Not because of the sites you were on or the conversations you were having, but simply because you were logged on. Most internet users are unaware of the dangers that lurk behind the screen, but with internet use and cyber attacks gaining rampant speed, it is crucial to understand why EVERYONE needs cybersecurity.

A simple password, an outdated antivirus or an unsecured wifi network are the threats of the 21st century. Are you prepared to protect your information?

What is Cybersecurity?

Cyber security is the practice of protecting information technology (IT), combating threats that work to steal, tarnish or manipulate information. It can come from inside or outside an organization and can affect individuals, large organizations and everything in between.

While individuals can be affected by various threats, an individual's laptop or phone is rarely used as an exploited device. Business' central servers are typically what's impacted, taking devices offline. This, in turn, stops business operations in their tracks, costing large sums of money due to lost time, and this is on top of any financial damage an actual hacker might demand.

Common Cyber security Threats

When it comes to cyber security, there's a wide range of threats or attacks we see on a regular basis. Evaluating these threats will allow you to stay on top of your own cyber security and avoid having your business' information stolen or altered.

Ransomware

Ransomware is one of the most common cyber security threats. Its attack is centered around stopping access to personal files or a system until a ransom payment is made in exchange. Hackers encrypt the information, making it completely inaccessible without the use of a decryption key.

This type of attack is what was happening in our opening story. It can be incredibly harmful to a small business, especially if the attackers threaten to destroy your data if the ransom is not paid. The threat usually occurs through malicious spam such as links to websites or attachments that when opened, attack your system.

Malware

Another common threat is known as malware. It's also known as "malicious software" and it's any number of malicious programs that could infect your system in the hopes of stealing or corrupting data. When speaking of malware, worms, viruses, trojans, and spyware are the terms most often used. They're often seen as an unsafe download or email attachment that's created by a team of hackers.

These attacks often have the ability to fly below the radar of familiar detection methods such as antivirus tools, making them more dangerous. That means that even if you're using tools that specifically search for tainted files, these software variants can take over computer access, potentially causing a great deal of damage.

Distributed Denial of Service (DDoS)

Botnet attacks and Distributed Denial of Service (DDoS) are other types of cyber attacks. They usually work hand-in-hand to threaten security. A botnet is when a network of bots across a range of computers are infected and can be controlled remotely. Bots are often used in DDoS attacks in order to crash a server, for example.

What makes these types of attacks so dangerous is that the hacker could be using your computer along with a chain of others in order to carry out the attack. These attacks rely on a high CPU and memory use to crash an application, which is why many computers are needed.

Man-in-the-Middle (MitM)

The man-in-the-middle (MitM) attack is also a common cyber threat. It involves a two-party transaction where one of the hackers interrupts traffic while the other steals the data. This is commonly seen when using public WiFi that isn't secure and attackers can access information without you knowing. It can also occur when a device already has malware and a hacker installs software to gain access to the victim's information.

Phishing

Phishing is the act of sending spam emails from what appears to be a reliable email. Phishing emails usually contain a strong and compelling subject line, encouraging the person receiving the email to open it. It could be a potential job offer containing attachments to make it more believable.

Phishing is one of the most common cyber attacks, its purpose is to steal data such as bank account or credit card information. While email filtering technologies can be set up to help avoid these emails, it's also important to be aware of preventative measures you can implement yourself in case you come across one.

One of the easiest ways to decrease the chances of a phishing attack is implementing two-factor authentication. Even if a hacker has your password, two-factor makes it significantly harder for them to access your information.

Although these are threats you'll see often, it's important to remember that cyber attacks are continually evolving and become more innovative quite rapidly. Due to their constant evolution, secure systems can still be hacked. Having a proper cyber security system in place is the only way to protect important data or information as best as possible.

Types of Cybersecurity

In order to avoid cyber crime, a cyber security strategy is essential. Protection often comes in the form of many layers, to minimize or eliminate the possibility of destroyed or altered data, disruption to business operations, or extortion of money.

Some cyber security methods include:

- Application Security - Security features are built into applications when they're being designed. This type of security takes many aspects into consideration in order to protect information while being used and when it's in the cloud.

- Data Security - When working to ensure data is secure, data storage systems are designed to keep the information safe when it's being stored, as well as while it's in transit.
- Network Security - Hardware and software systems are put in place to protect a network from internal and external threats. This stops misuse or unauthorized access from happening.
- Mobile Security - It's crucial that businesses that use mobile devices protect the information from threats.
- Cloud Security - The cloud is used to store large sums of data. In order to properly protect it, it must be encrypted when at rest, in motion, and while it's in use.
- Information Security - This type of security is used for protecting your most sensitive data. Measures such as the General Data Protection Regulation (GDRP) maintain a high level of security.
- Critical Infrastructure Security - This type of security is necessary when protecting large networks that support greater society, that affect public safety, national security, or economic health.

Cybersecurity Myths

With so much information online regarding cyber security, it can be challenging to know what's true or not. Aside from online information, many people create false beliefs in their own minds when it comes to cyber security. This can be incredibly dangerous because, without proper information, you may make choices that will affect the security of yourself and your personal information.

One of the biggest misconceptions about cybersecurity is that cyber criminals are outsiders. While some cyber threats do come from outside an organization, it's not uncommon to come across threats working within an organization — by themselves, or in a group or partnership with outside hackers.

Another cyber security myth is believing that a certain industry is less at risk than others. While risks vary from one industry to another, hackers don't discriminate. Small businesses or large, private or government-run organizations, all are at risk of facing threats online.

The digital world is greatly connected to our physical world. Unfortunately, many fail to understand how they are linked and how it's related to cyber security. Many physical items used in business are now controlled digitally, and when invaded by hackers, this not only results in a loss of information but can also affect your physical world. Just think about the public transit system and how a breach in their security could result in anything from an inconvenience to a catastrophic event.

Many people also believe that using antivirus software is enough to protect themselves. Sure, it's helpful in detecting some viruses, but hackers have found their way around these software systems and have successfully hidden their attacks from their victims for months at a time while they steal or damage information.

Issues with Modern Cybersecurity Products

As previously mentioned, hackers are continuously changing and growing as technology does the same. This has made it challenging for cyber security products to stay on top of these criminals. The regulation process for modern cyber security products is far too slow and by the time they are regulated and available, they don't do a great job at fighting off various threats.

It's also become more challenging to sort through data, with attackers going after the data integrity itself and causing long-term damage to an individual's or group's data. The emergence of AI has been helpful in trying to sort and check data integrity but it's still a work in progress.

Staying Safe with Cybersecurity

Although using the internet comes with many risks, there are many ways in which an individual or business can protect themselves and their information online. By implementing a cyber security system, you lessen the risk of losing valuable content or assets. There are many options available depending on specific needs and they only require a few steps to arrange.

Steps to Protecting Yourself: Understand, Educate and Secure

Firstly, adopt a risk management strategy. Understanding the risk allows to prioritize, document, and communicate to raise awareness.

Secondly, invest in awareness and education. This responsibility is not solely on the IT team, but it is important for the CEO and staff involved to learn their personal security responsibilities and cyber risks.

And finally, but not limited to, securing the IT infrastructure and protecting the perimeter. Be sure to create and maintain policies, deploy, and implement tools such as two-factor authentication and firewalls.

It's no longer a matter of "if," but "when" you'll be attacked, which is why cyber security is critical. Having a prevention mindset is incredibly important when hoping to eliminate both known and unknown threats!

Sources:

https://www.secureworldexpo.com/industry-news/ransomware-when-companies-pay-hackers-do-they-get-their-data-back#:~:text=Proofpoint%20researchers%20found%20that%20nearly,got%20access%20to%20their%20data.

https://www.ibm.com/topics/cybersecurity

https://www.stanfieldit.com/cyber-security-threats/

https://www.cisco.com/c/en/us/products/security/common-cyberattacks.html#~types-of-cyber-attacks

https://geekflare.com/understanding-cybersecurity/

https://nexthop.ca/it-news/what-is-cybersecurity-and-how-does-it-work/

https://www.forbes.com/sites/williamsaito/2017/04/04/these-are-10-cybersecurity-myths-that-must-be-busted/?sh=5a1d8fe566ea

https://www.cybersecurityintelligence.com/blog/2020-top-issues-in-cyber-security--4721.html

About the Author

Felipe Isaza is a Cybersecurity and Information Technology Expert with 16+ years of experience in a variety of different business markets.

In 2011, Felipe founded FUNCSHUN, a managed it services and cybersecurity provider based out of Miami, Florida where he and his team are dedicated to helping business's securing their data in this ever-evolving cybersecurity threat landscape with an unprecedented 99% client retention rate over the past 10 years. FUNCSHUN is a Microsoft partner that primarily focuses on delivering trust and solutions in Cybersecurity, Risk Mitigation & Management, Managed IT Support, Cloud, and VoIP services to small and medium sized businesses in various professional industries. Prior to founding FUNCSHUN, Felipe worked for several companies as an IT Director and IT Manager in different industries allowing him to acquire the knowledge needed to enable his firm to provide the technology solutions needed to help manage customers risk, in addition to proactively educating and training himself and his team to stay ahead of the ever-evolving cybersecurity and technology trends.

Are you concerned about security? Book a strategy call with Felipe here:

https://1x1.felipeisaza.com

https://www.linkedin.com/in/felipe-isaza/

https://www.facebook.com/feli.isaza

Real Life Hacks

Greg Mullen

The cybersecurity minefield mentioned in this book's title didn't exist 25 years ago. It's not something that business owners, entrepreneurs, or MBA programs talked about. The topic of business risk as a broader field has always been an area of careful consideration. Ultimately, the problems and solutions to cyber security threats are the same as any threat from one group to another and must be solved in the same way, with law enforcement and criminal justice. However, the digital landscape is still very much a new frontier, and just like in the days of the Wild, Wild West, governments and law enforcement agencies struggle to catch and prosecute outlaw criminal gangs that continue to harm and threaten society.

Constitutional rule of law with well-defined and protected property rights, even when imperfect provides a foundational political structure for the market economy, increasing standards of living. This very system is under threat as the global internet fuels the information revolution. However, it is simultaneously limiting the ability of authorities to protect businesses and citizens from cyber threats and attacks.

ABQ-IT, the IT managed services company that I co-founded, is headquartered in Albuquerque, New Mexico, the state famous for the likes of Billy the Kid and other outlaw gangs looking to cause chaos and escape justice. But Billy the Kid and Old West gangs couldn't have ever fleeced the state and escaped justice like cyber-criminals have in the past few years. The sheer number of state and government entities hit by cyber criminals is staggering, along with the dollar amounts. And justice? Forget about it. Very few cases ever get to trial, with criminal gangs residing in countries not generally friendly with the US and where no extradition treaties or means to seek or pursue arrest exist. With little to zero enforcement options, businesses and government organizations in New Mexico turn to companies like ABQ-IT to focus on prevention and mitigation strategies that are proven to help in the face of relentless and increasing cyber attacks.

Obviously, the problem extends much farther than just in one state. Part of the issue here is that it can be really difficult to estimate how large of a problem cyber attacks are: most attacks on private businesses go unreported, leaving only public corporations and government entities to dominate the news cycles. Not surprisingly, most businesses aren't eager to advertise that they had a cyber security issue and the media only reports on it when it causes a problem too large to ignore.

At the time of writing, the United States was still reeling from the largest cyber attack on the energy sector in history. On Friday April 7th, 2021, multiple news agencies, including the New York Times,[7] reported that Colonial Pipeline had closed its entire 5,500-mile conduit carrying gasoline and other fuels from the Gulf Coast to the New York metro area. The company was attempting to contain a ransomware attack perpetrated on its IT infrastructure. News of the Colonial Pipeline attack dominated the headlines; while the pipeline company worked around the clock with government agencies to restore their systems from the crippling ransomware incident. The news was filled with pictures of cars lining up at gas stations as the entire East Coast of the United States scrambled for fuel.

The Colonial Pipeline attack represents a long list of escalating, malicious cyber attacks carried out against private US businesses and government entities that go far beyond causing chaos in the digital world and lost dollars. The effect was real-life pain, panic, discomfort, and even lives lost.

---

[7] https://www.nytimes.com/2021/05/08/us/politics/cyberattack-colonial-pipeline.html

A private company, Colonial Pipeline is, according to their website[8] at the time of writing this, "the largest refined products pipeline in the United States, transporting more than 100 million gallons of fuel daily to meet the energy needs of consumers from Houston, Texas to the New York Harbor."

According to the updates on their website, it took five days for the pipeline to come back online and another week for the delivery supply chain to get back to normal operations. And the damage ripples through society, going far beyond the monetary, although the monetary figures themselves are staggering. According to the Bloomberg article, "Colonial Pipeline Paid Hackers Nearly $5 Million in Ransom," the company not only paid out the hackers, but also affected a devastating economic fallout resulting from the shutdown.

Uncertainty makes people behave in unpredictable and sometimes, irrational ways. For example, the US. Consumer Product Safety Commission warned people in a Tweet "...not [to] fill plastic bags with gasoline. Use only containers approved for fuel." Other ripples, like the images flashing across the screen of a burned-out Hummer. The driver had loaded his vehicle with approved containers full of gas, but after leaving the gas station, an explosion, totaled the vehicle and injured himself and an occupant.

---

[8] https://www.colpipe.com/about-us

The Colonial Pipeline cyber attack was ultimately tied to an eastern European, likely Russian-associated criminal gang known as Darkside.

One report from ZDNET[9] describes Darkside as:

"...believed to be relatively new to the ransomware scene, first spotted in the summer of 2020, Darkside has already created a leak website used in double-extortion campaigns, in which victim companies are not only locked out of their systems, but also have their information stolen.

If these organizations refuse to pay up, stolen data may be published on the platform and made available to the public.

Darkside isn't just content in making money from ransomware demands, however, as the group has indicated it will happily work with competitors or investors before leaks are published."

The ZDNET report continues to directly quote the group:

"'If the company refuses to pay, we are ready to provide information before the publication, so that it would be possible to earn in the reduction price of shares,' the group says."

In other words, the gang is willing to share insider information to help competitors or inside traders

---

9 https://www.zdnet.com/article/colonial-pipeline-ransomware-attack-everything-you-need-to-know

profit or short sell stock based on information that the group has yet to publish.

Even worse, the type of ransomware being sold by groups like Darkside includes a leak-website, which is a public internet domain where they'll publish private information on compromised businesses. Leak-websites make it much more than a technical problem and more of a PR and a legal one. Even if a business manages to restore all of their technical infrastructure, they now have the problem of confidential information published to the public domain and controlled entirely by the hackers who will only remove the information if they have their demands met. And demand amounts are increasing according to a report[10] late last year from Coveware: the average ransomware payment in the third quarter of 2020 was $233,817, up 31%from the second quarter of 2019.

The Colonial Pipeline attack illustrates that these attacks have real-world consequences that go far beyond the digital or the monetary. They cause human suffering, pain and destruction, forever changing lives for the worst.

The US government needs to modernize its thinking and methods in extracting justice for the victims of cyber crime. The government needs to implement a

---

[10] https://www.coveware.com/blog/q3-2020-ransomware-marketplace-report#:~:text=Average%20Ransomware%20Increases%20as%20Attackers%20Target%20Bigger%20Companies&text=The%20average%20ransom%20payment%20increased,to%20drag%20the%20averages%20up.

coordinated response and aggressive, offensive counter-measures designed to disrupt and remove the ability to cause harm to US businesses and individuals. Until then, businesses, state and local governments can work with companies like ABQ-IT to develop a better cyber security posture, utilizing state-of-the-art technologies and human talent to prevent, detect, and neutralize threats. Following, we then create a robust business continuity and incident threat response plan to take action if an attack breaks through.

Even with all of the above security measures, cyber gangs still have the statistical advantage. This is one of the reasons why offensive measures are needed — hackers only have to succeed once to cause serious damage. This fact has given rise to the cyber insurance industry helping to tackle this risk. Insurance has been widely used as an effective risk-mitigation strategy. Though the specific and nuanced field of cyber insurance is new, the methods insurance companies use to make it into a viable business model are well understood. For example, insurance companies are dealing with the increase in claims with heightened scrutiny on gross negligence, denying claims when covered entities ignore best practices for achieving a basic level of cyber hygiene.

For a list of 15 ways to protect your business from cyber attacks please visit our website at www.abq-it.com.

About the Author

Born in Albuquerque, New Mexico, Greg Mullen has made New Mexico his home for most of his life and participating in activities like riding horses and hunting elk high up in the mountains. He was raised with a strong work ethic and entrepreneurial spirit.

Having co-founded several companies Greg can be called a serial entrepreneur and passionate business owner. He started his career in telecom sales and after a decade in various sales roles and industries including telecom and Greg co-founded Albuquerque Computer & Electronics Company (ACER) in 2008 specializing in end-of-life IT asset management (ITAD) and quickly positioning the company as the leading provider in the U.S. South West where it remains today with Greg as the company President.

In 2012 Greg moved with his wife Vanessa to Austin, Texas where he undertook Enterprise Account Management roles while remaining a board-member and owner of ACER but removed from the day-to-day interactions. In Austin, Greg had the pleasure of working with clients like Disney, NASA Jet Propulsion

Labs on a variety of projects from IT infrastructure to software consulting before again getting involved as a co-founder in two companies, one of which ABQ-IT eventually brought him, Vanessa and now their 4 year old son Ethan back to New Mexico to be President of both ACER and ABQ-IT, where Greg and his family remain today.

Outside of running two companies, Greg and Vanessa enjoy homeschooling Ethan and participating in family outings to the mountain for skiing, or in the mesa chasing hot air balloons or playing various musical instruments such as violin, piano or guitar.

Understanding the Impact of the Dark Web

By Raj Sidhu

The dark web is not something that the average person understands but it should be a very serious concern for both the private and public sector. In recent years, it has redefined the art of hacking, and, in the process, dramatically expanded the threat landscape that organizations now face. So, what exactly is the dark web and how does it impact all of us?

The dark web is a collection of thousands of websites that cannot be accessed via normal internet browsers. These websites are also not indexed by search engines like Google or Bing, making them inaccessible to the general public.

In simple terms, the dark web is an overlay of networks that requires special tools and software to gain access — not very difficult to do. The history of the dark web predates the 80s; back then, the term was originally used to describe computers on ARPANET (the old internet). This network was hidden from the public and programmed to receive messages but remained invisible or in the dark.

Since then, the word "dark web" has evolved into an umbrella term that describes the side of the internet purposefully not open to anyone —hidden networks whose architecture is superimposed on that of the internet.

Like most projects of this scope, the dark web's evolution can be traced back to the US military. The most common way to access the dark web is through using tools like Tor. The network routing capability utilized by the Tor network was developed in the mid-90s by mathematicians and computer scientists at the US Naval Research Laboratory, with the purpose of protecting US intelligence communications online.

The dark web is used in various ways including email, sharing files, and hosting news and e-commerce websites. Accessing it requires specific software, configurations, or authorization, often using non-standard communication protocols and ports. Currently, two of the most popular ways to access the dark web are through two overlay networks: the aforementioned Tor, and I2P.

Tor stands for “the onion router” or “onion routing.” Tor is designed to keep its user base anonymous. Just like the layers of an onion, data is stored within multiple layers of encryption. Each layer reveals the next relay until the final layer sends the data to its destination. Information is sent bidirectionally, so data is being sent back and forth via the same tunnel. On any given day, over one million users are active on the Tor network.

I2P stands for the Invisible Internet Project. It is designed for user-to-user file sharing and collaboration. It takes data and encapsulates it within multiple layers, therefore encrypting your data and making it nearly impossible for anyone to snoop. Just like a clove of garlic, information is bunched together with other people’s information to prevent de-packing and inspection, and data is sent through a unidirectional tunnel.

As discussed earlier, the dark web is used for news, e-commerce sites, and email and hosting services. While many of the services are innocent (might be legal and are simply alternatives to what can be found on the lighter side of the internet), a portion of the dark web is tied to illegal activities due to its promise of anonymity. Since the 90s, cyber criminals have found a new home on the dark web as a way to communicate, coordinate, and monetize the art of cyber attacks.

One of the most popular ways for us humans to communicate is through email, which explains the increased popularity in ransomware attacks. Cyber criminals often send phishing emails designed to look like legitimate emails which will lure the end-user into providing their credentials, banking credentials, or other important personal details. These credentials and details are collected and subsequently sold on forums through the dark web. This is why it is important to have active dark web scans running for your email domain so that you can actively address compromises when they are reported on the dark web.

Nearly every cyber crime has a financial motive and we have recently seen cyber criminals become more effective because of new and easy-to-use tools. We have also started to see a collaboration between cyber criminals where they use leaked data from multiple sources to create databases. For example, if you were part of the 2016 LinkedIn data breach, you were one of 117 million users whose passwords and other important details were stolen and subsequently sold on the dark web. Every day, I read about private companies disclosing details of their data breaches and it scares me to find how negligent these organizations were in protecting consumer data.

Similar to cloud computing that enterprises might use as part of their technology infrastructure, dark web hosting services are leveraged by cyber criminals and hackers. Dark web hosting services host websites or e-commerce marketplaces that sell distributed denial-of-service (DDoS) tools and services. These hosting services are typically very unstable as they can be "taken down" by law enforcement or vigilante hackers for political, ideological, or moral reasons.

Forums also exist to allow hackers and criminals independent discussions for the purpose of knowledge exchange, organizing and coordinating DDoS campaigns (such as those planned by the infamous hacker group known as Anonymous), and/or exchanging cyber attack best practices. These forums come with a variety of technical options and languages and can be associated with particular threat actors/groups, hacktivists, attack vectors, etc. This is also where your stolen email/domain credentials can be sold and bought easily with cryptocurrency.

Like the lighter side of the internet, there are dark web search engines: Candle and Torch are the two most commonly used. These search engines allow users to easily locate and navigate various forums, sites, and e-commerce stores just like Google or Bing do.

Perhaps more than any other service usage, e-commerce sites on the dark web have exploded in popularity in recent years due to the rise of both DDoS as a service and stresser services. The result is huge profit margins for hackers leveraging their unique skills to create a market. Everything from DDoS attack tools and botnet rentals to "contracting" the services of a hacker are now available on the dark web for the right price in cryptocurrency. All the while, the dark web promises complete anonymity.

So, what does this mean? Well, these e-commerce sites and their products have commoditized cyber attacks in addition to making them available to a wide range of non-technical users. This is one of the reasons why 75% of organizations around the world experienced some kind of phishing attack in 2020.[11] Oftentimes, these services come with easy-to-follow, easy-to-use interfaces that make setting up and launching cyber attacks quick and easy for cyber criminals just launching their careers.

Stressers

For example, Putinstresser is a recent DDoS-as-a-service tool and is one of the newest additions to the growing array of low-priced services commonly known as "booter" or "stresser" services. These services provide potential buyers with various payment options, discovery tools, a variety of attack vectors, and even chat-based customer support. Botnet rental services are also available — their growth has paralleled the growth and use of botnets since 2016. An example of a botnet service available on the dark web is the JenX botnet which was discovered in 2018. The JenX botnet can find and infect internet of things (IoT) devices with specific vulnerabilities on the internet and provide the hacker with control of the device. (IoT is a system of interrelated computing

---

11 https://www.graphus.ai/blog/10-facts-about-phishing-in-2021-that-you-need-to-see

devices used across many applications in consumer, commercial, and defense.)

IoT Hacking Tools

Prices for IoT hacking tools are as diverse as the attack vectors available for purchase, some for as little as $20. Prices are typically based on various factors, such as the number of attack vectors included within the service, the size of the attack, and the demand.

Malware & Ransomware

Malware and ransomware are equally popular. The notorious WannaCry global ransomware campaign had its servers hosted on the dark web. In addition, just like their botnet and DDoS brethren, malware and ransomware have their own "as-a-service" services, which dramatically simplifies the process of launching a ransomware campaign. Numerous ransomware services exist that allow a user to pick the ransom amount and add notes/letters. The user is provided with a simple executable to send to victims.

There is a plethora of dark web services available, giving nearly anyone with access to the dark web the ability to contract hackers or other nefarious cybercriminals for their work. Use of cryptocurrency has made this a very simple process in the virtual world.

The global community is starting to see the impact of the dark web on a daily basis through the news. It seems like every week we are seeing one organization after another get compromised. All of these criminal activities are being attributed to cyber criminals that have the ability to organize on the dark web, create, and distribute cyber attacks all over the world. There are now databases of citizens being maintained on the dark web with much of our personal data: first names, last names, physical addresses, email addresses, date of birth, social security numbers, security questions. This data is the aggregation of all compromises. Your personal data is valuable and the cyber criminals will try to steal and financially benefit from it.

So, what does this mean for us?

Steps For Cleaning Up Your Cyber Security

These are some basic steps everyone should take to ensuring a greater cyber hygiene that results in lower chances of your data being compromised:

1. Use MFA
    a. Using MFA reduces your chances of being compromised exponentially
2. Use strong passwords (12 characters or longer)
    a. Use a phrase
3. Use auto-created strong, lengthy, cryptic passwords
4. Use password managers
    a. It does not matter which one
    b. Make sure it is encrypted
5. Use a throwaway email for all "junk"

a. Using your email for registering with third-party websites or applications exposes you to breaches should they arise. Never use work email to register for non-work-related accounts or apps. Homechef .com was forced to admit a data breach after 8 million records belonging to the site were being sold on the dark web, including passwords. Most users use the same password for all or most of their apps or websites, which results in further data breaches.

6. Use a dark web scanning and monitoring tool
   a. You want to be aware and react if and when your data shows up on the dark web.
7. Limit-privileged users
   a. Use standard user accounts for all normal tasks
8. Classify and protect your data
   a. Verify data permissions
   b. Verify multi-tiered backup and restore process
   c. Encrypt your data
9. Be aware of what you post publicly

A Light Shines

However, not all is doom and gloom. We now have multi-factor authentication (MFA), a simple and effective step in tightening cyber security. All applications and services should require multi-factor authentication for all devices, applications, and services. A single username/password combo is not enough protection from cyber criminals anymore.

In light of all the recent cyber criminal activity, the United States government is starting to take cyber crime seriously; as I am writing this chapter, President Joe Biden has signed an Executive Order to require MFA for all accounts that work with the government, along with many other requirements to increase level of security measures.

The European Union has been ahead of the United States in addressing digital privacy and data ownership concerns. General Data Protection Regulation (GDPR) was enacted into law by the European Union (EU) in 2018. GDPR provides a greater level of protection and privacy for EU citizens by requiring companies to abide by strict guidelines for their computing environments. In the US, California, New York, and other states have followed suit by enacting their version of the regulation. As a cyber security professional, I know we will be very busy for years to come.

About the Author

Raj Sidhu is the Founder and CEO of inTech Consulting, a Managed Security and Services Provider based in the Pacific Northwest.

inTech Consulting provides Managed I.T. Services to small and medium sized business throughout the United States. inTech also provides cybersecurity and compliance management as a service for their clients.

Raj has over 20 years of experience in technology industry, along with the past 7 years serving as the President of inTech. Raj earned a

bachelor's degree from Eastern Washington University and has several industry related certificates from Microsoft and one completed in 2020 from University of Washington: Certificate in Applied Cybersecurity.

Are Small Businesses More at Risk of Cyber Attack?

By Rob Downs

The answer to the title of this chapter is, "Yes." There, shortest chapter ever.

But you are not here for just yes/no answers. So let me explain... now time for the longest chapter ever.

There are two ways to evaluate this question. First, are small businesses more at risk of cyber attack in general? Second, are small businesses more at risk when compared to mid-sized and enterprise level businesses? The answer to both of those scenarios is, "Yes."

At one time, hackers only attacked larger, more lucrative targets. They worked diligently to get into a business' digital network to compromise them and score a big payday for their efforts. Anyone remember the Target hack from 2013?[12] Hackers were able to access the megastore's corporate system by hacking their HVAC monitoring system. With that, they got access to millions of credit card numbers and other customer data.

Today, things have changed. Now hackers are running tools to look for vulnerabilities all over the internet. They are using spambots to send emails with dangerous payloads, which are either links to dangerous websites or attachments that have malware built in. Millions of emails are sent every year with one purpose — to compromise a computer, get access to data, and encrypt the computer and other computers on the same network.

"But my business is too small," you say, "we don't have any money." Some of you might ask, "Who would ever target my company?"

You're right, cyber criminals might not specifically seek out your company, but who passes up several thousands of dollars if it's just sitting there for the taking? Hackers send out phishing emails, casting a wide net with the hopes that one of their recipients will take the bait. Maybe you or one of your employees just happens to click on the wrong thing or open the wrong attachment and BOOM, the hackers are in.

---

[12] https://www.reuters.com/article/us-target-breach/target-cyber-breach-hits-40-million-payment-cards-at-holiday-peak-idUSBRE9BH1GX20131219

Maybe you will get lucky, and they will just encrypt your computers and ask for a ransom payment. Or, they will scope out your business once they are in and try to get the passwords stored in your computers. Another tactic? They will monitor your computer to see what sites you go to, log all your keystrokes, and wait until they get the passwords to your online banking account. You were not targeted directly, but you became a quick score anyways.

In 2020, the average time from when a system was compromised to the discovery of the hack was 207 days.[13] Just think of what someone could do or learn about your company in that amount of time.

On the other hand, perhaps, they did target your company. Why? Because you're loaded? Probably not. Most often it's because they happened upon some credentials for your company on the dark web. All types of usernames and passwords are available for sale in marketplaces on the dark web. Passwords are a pain, I know. Having a different password for every site you use can be annoying, so you do like most people and reuse the same password. Over and over and over. So now a hacker has the password you use for your LinkedIn account (Remember that LinkedIn breach from 2012? Did you change your password after that?) Do you use that password for any other accounts? Perhaps you still use that password, not with LinkedIn, but with your personal Gmail account. Or an old credit

---

[13] https://enterprise.verizon.com/resources/reports/2021-data-breach-investigations-report.pdf

card account. It doesn't matter. As a bad guy, a hacker is going to try that username and password combination all over the internet. They can even get creative and have their software add a 1 to the end or maybe a 1 and an exclamation point. This hacker is a bad guy with a computer and some time, and can try all types of tricks.

You and your business are a target for the simple fact that you have a presence on the internet. That's all they need. And the bad guys know that with smaller companies, owners don't spend their budget on things like password managers for staff, or cyber security training, or spam filtering, or network monitoring, or backups. Most small businesses see cyber security as overly complicated or something that slows them or their employees down.

"We're small, we're nimble, we're fast," you think.

That's how many small businesses see themselves. And the bad guys know that, too.

The Need for Cyber Security Policies and Procedures

That leads to another reason that small businesses are targets. They don't have policies and procedures to deal with these types of attacks. Who has access to your bank accounts? Who can authorize a transfer or a change in payment accounts for accounts payable? Who can change bank routing numbers and accounts for paying your employees? Do you have policies in place with checks and balances to prevent any one person from having all the access?

I had a client a few years ago that got hacked because of a lack of policy and protections. (Unfortunately, they did not engage with us to work on their policies as it wasn't deemed an "IT Support" function. We now work with all clients to create policies.) They were targeted because email credentials were posted on the dark web. Within TWO weeks of the credentials being reported, their email system was compromised. The crooks were patient and redirected emails to an anonymous Gmail account. They watched for a few weeks and then made their move. They worked via email to convince the accounts payable (AP) person that they were one of the company's vendors and even bought a domain that was only one letter off. They created a rule in the AP person's email to redirect any emails sent to the vendor's correct domain to the bogus domain instead. After a few more weeks, the cyber criminals informed the AP person that they had changed their payment location and provided a new routing number and account number, asking the AP person to wire the outstanding balance due to this new account. It was close to $250,000.

Now you are thinking, that's how they will get tripped up. That bank account can be traced. Turns out that the receiving bank account was a compromised account of someone in Iowa who had their credentials stolen. I'm sure the plan was to get the transfer into that fake account and then immediately transfer it to some overseas account. My client got lucky; the receiving bank had a policy to hold funds for large inbound wire transfers and the business was able to recover their money.

This didn't have to happen at all; the client chose to be vulnerable (whether through ignorance or cost savings). Policy would have prevented this from happening. Two-factor authentication or multi-factor authentication would have stopped it. Monitoring changes in email rules on the server would have caught this. Having an active monitoring service on the dark web would have prevented this. A password policy that required changing passwords every 90 days might have helped. Many IT folks will tell you that they cannot protect you 100% — hackers only have to be right once to get in. But IT security has to be right all of the time. You can see from the list above that a good defensive strategy at any of several attack points would have stopped this hack dead in its tracks.

Looking for Your Clients, Not You

Another reason that your company may be targeted isn't because the cyber crooks want access to your systems. No, they want access to one of your clients. If they are after bigger fish, they will look at their true target and figure out who those targets do business with. That's you. It's much easier to get into a small business' systems than some large corporation's. Once they are in your network, then they just have to wait and see how you communicate with the larger company. If they are really lucky, you not only communicate with the larger company, but you have access to a special website, or even better, you have a direct connection via a VPN (virtual private network). Through your company, the hackers can get into the larger company's network and wreak havoc. And let's face it, once the hackers are done with you and get to their main prize, why wouldn't they also take you down, too? They are already in your network and have gathered all your information anyway.

Easy Risk, Easy Reward

Finally, the main reason that cyber criminals might target you over a larger company comes down to a great risk/reward ratio. The criminals know that if they target smaller companies for smaller amounts, then they will never get caught. If you get hacked or ransomed, the police won't or can't do anything for you.

I know what you are thinking, "Certainly, the FBI can help?"

They might be able to, but there are so many hacks and too few resources. The FBI or Secret Service will not get involved with anything less than $3,000,000. You might not have millions sitting around in the bank, but I bet once or twice a month, you have a decent amount of money sitting in your payroll account or you get a large payment from a client. When you think about it, that amount is not a bad pay day for several hours work for a cyber criminal.

The biggest take away from this chapter is: ***this does not have to happen to you.***

There are tools available for you and your business to make you less of a target and stop these crooks. It may seem daunting at first, even overwhelming, but as the old adage goes, "How do you eat an elephant? One bite at a time." Take one step at a time. Add one policy at a time, one new tool at a time. And if you don't understand it, then talk to your IT support folks. They can help you formulate a plan to move forward and implement steps, it's what they do. They stay current on the ever-changing tricks hackers use and how best to keep them out, so you don't have to become an expert in your spare time.

Set expectations for your staff that they (and you, no exceptions!) must start using these new tools, adhering to the new policies, and taking your company's cyber security training seriously. It's necessary for the security measures to work, but a tool not used, or used improperly may as well not be used at all.

Unfortunately, most small businesses that suffer a cyber security attack or breach close their doors within six months of the attack. You don't want that to be you. Your employees certainly don't want the stress of finding a new job. So, as mentioned, start with one layer and build, don't stop at just one tool. Securing your business from cyber attacks is just like securing anything else. One layer is good, but several layers are better, just like bean dip.

About the Author

Rob Downs, Cyber Security Expert and Chief Technology Strategist

Rob Downs has been in the IT industry for over 25 years and has owned Palladium Networks since 2001. Palladium Networks acquired Managed IT Solutions in 2014. He has grown the company from a basic IT support firm to a provider of cloud services and then a leading Cyber Security firm.

Before forming his own company, Rob worked for other IT firms from a small computer firm to a Fortune 100 powerhouse. Based on his experience at these other firms, Rob built his company with a customer service priority while providing quality service.

When not working on his company, Rob likes to tinker with his own personal computer systems and spend time with his family on the coast of North Carolina. He has also served on the boards of local community non-profits.

Why Your Business is Vulnerable to Hackers

By Randy Bryan

A few years ago, I received a panicky phone call from an executive at a regional, mid-sized construction company. About a week earlier, one of their long-term employees had opened a malicious email and clicked on the link it contained. Within minutes, the employee's computer was encrypted and was asking for a ransom. On top of that, the company's shared folders were also encrypted and also waiting on a ransom.

The company had never heard of my company (tekRESCUE) and had first called the local computer guy in their small town. The computer guy spent a week trying to break the encryption on the files and in the process broke the encryption itself. This meant there was no way the files could be recovered, even if they paid the ransom. In frustration, they fired the computer guy and called us.

Once we took over, we saw how grim the situation was. The company didn't have an IT person, just an employee volunteering to do it on the side. They had no recent backups. The server and the employee's computer had to be wiped. The other employees didn't really trust the volunteer IT person, so some of the employees had copies of their own work. This turned out to be a stroke of good luck because it was data we could recover.

We were able to get everything back to normal in about two weeks so the company was down three weeks total. The sad thing is that once we got them back to normal, they chose to keep their volunteer IT person. Most likely, the company will get hacked again; statistics trend that way. It's just a matter of time.

The above story is just one of the many times we have seen this type of scenario play out. The current cybersecurity landscape is rapidly changing, and it's understandably becoming harder for businesses to keep up. Just a few years ago, we could talk about "if" your business

would ever be hit by a cyber attack. Times have changed. Now we talk about "when" your business will be hit. Many business owners are shocked when they hear this from me: your business isn't immune to a cyber attack.

As we speak, your business is vulnerable to a cyber attack for many reasons. Some of these deal with the motivation of the attackers, some have to do with the current realities of cybersecurity, and some of them deal with vulnerabilities in your business. In this chapter we want to examine all of these.

You're Vulnerable Because Cyber Crime is Way Up

I cannot understate the transformation currently happening in cyber crime. Presently, it is growing faster than it has at any other point in history. We saw a huge increase in cyber crime from 2010-2020, and in 2020 it just seemed to explode exponentially. One of the greatest indicators of growth of cyber crime is the growth of the cybersecurity industry to meet it. In recent history, we have already seen:

- A huge increase in yearly spending on cybersecurity, from $4.5 billion in 2004[14] to $167 billion in 2020[15]. Growth is expected to continue with a rate of at least 10% year over year. It is predicted to reach $372 billion globally by 2028.[16]

---

[14] Cybercrime Magazine, 2019, https://cybersecurityventures.com/cybersecurity-market-report

[15] Grandview Research, 2021, https://www.grandviewresearch.com/industry-analysis/cyber-security-market

[16] Ibid

• In 2015, cyber crime cost the globe nearly $3 trillion yearly. In 2021, this number is expected to reach $6 trillion.[17]

Current predictions are that this number will increase to at least $10.5 trillion in 2025.[18] This is the long-term trend that we must fight against and ensure we prepare for. With an ever-growing number of tools for hackers to use, the rise of digital data, and the explosion of artificial intelligence being used for hacks, the threat is now bigger than ever.

The situation in 2020 grew even crazier, a trend that continued into 2021. The pandemic caused many people to adopt "Work from Home" (WFH) situations, or hybrid situations — working from the office some of the time and at home the rest of the time. All of this change increased the attack exposure for companies and their data. In the first quarter of 2020 alone, breaches were up over 267% compared to the same time in 2019.[19] The United Nations placed the rise in phishing attacks in 2020 alone at 600%.[20]

This trend will only increase in intensity and means that workers and their devices will become crucial endpoints in protecting against attack. During this

---

[17] Cybercrime Magazine, 2020, https://cybersecurityventures.com/cybercrime-damage-costs-10-trillion-by-2025

[18] Ibid

[19] CNBC, 2020, https://www.cnbc.com/2020/07/29/cybercrime-ramps-up-amid-coronavirus-chaos-costing-companies-billions.html

[20] ABC reporting on UN Report, 2020, https://abcnews.go.com/Health/wireStory/latest-india-reports-largest single-day-virus-spike-70826542

time of transition and change, there is often confusion and it is that confusion that cyber criminals take advantage of to thrive.

People Are Your Biggest Vulnerability

Often when I'm discussing cybersecurity with a business owner, they will say to me, “I'm too small to get hit with a ransomware attack,” or, "I'm just a _________ company, there's really nothing here worth taking from us." But nothing could be further from the truth. I recently had a good example of this play out for one of my clients.

Laura (not her real name) is on the executive team at a successful central Texas law firm. One day recently, she was having a productive phone discussion with a client. To move her client forward, she would need some information from her. They agreed on the info and hung up. Minutes later, an email popped into Laura's inbox from her client. Without even thinking, Laura clicked on the email and opened the attachment. Nothing happened. Laura took a second glance and realized the email was not legit. She quickly closed everything and deleted the email. That was her second mistake (not telling anybody). Her third mistake was waiting until the next day to reach out to our team about the issue. She called us when a seemingly unrelated issue popped up on her computer. While diagnosing that issue, my team discovered her email from the day before and what had transpired.

The good news is that after almost two hours of diagnosis and digital forensics, we determined that her security software blocked her attempts to open the malicious file and no compromise occurred.

But this brings me to my second important point: Your business is vulnerable to attacks because it is staffed by people. The above scenario plays out every single day. Often it does not have the happy ending that Laura experienced. Some of the biggest attacks in the past year have started the same way this story started. The main thing you need to understand is that it takes only one good-hearted and well-meaning employee to click on a link and bring your whole business to its knees... or maybe to an end.

Systems and processes are desperately needed that allow for and mitigate the vulnerability of people. Security software needs to be in place to mitigate the risk of bad links, email attachments, threat footholds, and other known attack vectors. We are under a constant cyber threat barrage and need the help that comes from having the right strategies. The problem is as businesses we have to "do business." Our security needs to stay out of the way as much as possible. Also, no security is 100% foolproof. That's why we desperately need training for our employees and executive staff. In the past, most people reading this would think “I have antivirus, this doesn’t apply to me” but the reality is that in the current climate, that’s not nearly enough.

Training, Training, Training

Even with every possible security mitigation strategy in place you can still have human error. That's why it's so important to implement an ongoing and effective training strategy to raise cybersecurity awareness among your employees and executive team. In as little as five minutes a week, you could mitigate attacks similar to one that happened to Laura. That attack got through their first line of defense. Thankfully, it was stopped by their second line of defense, but it could have been a horrible disaster. Cybersecurity training and simulated phishing training need to be implemented in businesses ASAP.

In my own company, the first time we started this training we had two employees click on fake phishing links. One of our employees even turned down the automatically offered training. When my employees fell for the phishing emails, this was devastating for me, but I knew it was just the first step in a process of becoming more secure. Our software offers a short, one minute training video to the offender if they click on one of the simulated phishing links. Within a couple of rounds of phishing training, we got to the place where nobody ever clicked on the links or opened the emails. Now, when one of my employees gets a suspicious email, they will take a screenshot and post it in our company chat. They do this to warn their fellow employees and to sometimes make fun of the criminals.

That first training event was a real eye opener, but we had to start somewhere! It's TRAINING that got us to this point and it's training that every business needs to reduce attack exposure in this vulnerable area of their business. When you have implemented successful training, employees will not only be able to detect threats, but also actively implement cybersecurity best practices.

Your Technology Makes You A Target

Your business is also vulnerable to attack because you use technology. It's a double-edged sword that can cut deep. In our world, we need technology to get our work done, but this same technology also makes us vulnerable to attacks.

First, there is the hardware we use. From smartphones, to laptops, to servers and printers and everything in between, everything we own now is interconnected. And with the transition to remote working, this has only become more pronounced. In an office setting, all it takes is one device getting compromised for your entire network and business to get breached.

Beyond the hardware you use, your business is vulnerable because you use software. One of the most recent examples of this vulnerability was the Microsoft Exchange servers hack of early 2021. These servers control a sizable portion of the world's email. Their vulnerabilities were exploited as a result of the SolarWinds® Orion hack a few months earlier. If you use these servers there is a high probability that cyber criminals got into your network.

Web server software is also commonly attacked. In 2018, Facebook had an estimated 30 million accounts-worth of data stolen. If it can happen to them, it can happen to you. Sometimes tools themselves become compromised and can infect anyone who uses them. Sometimes all it takes is one old account from a forum or business tool that you used years ago, and your password is compromised. This can lead to losing access to an account that is integral to your business.

NIST To The Rescue

The reality is that your business is vulnerable if you do not have good cybersecurity control processes in place. The best practices to put in place are those outlined in the NIST (National Institute of Standards) cybersecurity guidelines. The details of NIST are covered in other chapters of this book so I won't get into it too deeply here beyond the basics. What I will do is emphasize that these controls go hand in hand with your employee training and are part of a bigger picture. Laws, directives, and insurance guidelines are quickly coming our way which will require your business to be NIST compliant. I cannot stress this enough. If you are not adhering to the NIST guidelines very soon, you most likely will be crossing legal, compliance, or insurance lines that you do not want to cross.

Here's a quick list of the basics you need to be NIST compliant:

- training
- antivirus
- traffic monitoring
- intrusion detection
- threat hunting
- multi-factor authentication
- at-rest and in-travel encryption
- zero trust
- BYOD policies
- device-use policies
- disaster recovery plans and procedures
- incident response plan

And it goes without saying, you need an expert to help you understand and implement these controls.

The NIST guidelines are broken down into five sections: identify, protect, detect, respond, and recover. Here is how each section breaks down, simply put:

Identify

"Identify" is the first function laid out in the framework. It begins with identifying exactly what your business's core functions are and how they could be disrupted. This means determining where your business could be targeted, what assets you have that exist digitally, current risks, endpoints that are vulnerable, and tools used that could introduce the risk of a breach.

Protect

The next step, "Protect," means properly applying a defense set up by an expert, complete with the most up-to-date artificial intelligence to defend your business. Everything you identified as important to the function of your business needs to be protected.

Detect

The next section is "Detect." According to a report published by IBM in 2020, the average time to detect a breach is 207 days. How much damage could a hacker do to you if they saw everything you did within your business for 207 days? Once identified, it takes an average of 73 days to contain a threat. The longer this process goes on, the more costly it will be. Companies that manage to contain a breach in less than 200 days save a million dollars on average compared to those who do not.[21] This means having continuous detection strategies in place is paramount.

Respond

Next, "Respond" deals with your response to the threat and having someone formulate a plan to deal with the impact of a threat.

---

[21] IBM, 2020, https://www.ibm.com/security/data-breach

Recover

Finally, “Recover” deals with restoring full functionality to your business and making sure that the threat does not reassert itself to cripple your business again. Both need to be prepared far in advance so you will be ready “when” the time comes.

Blood, Sweat, and Tears

I was talking with a business owner recently about their lack of cybersecurity. She said some things that I hear shockingly often. She said that there's nothing in her business that anybody would want. She literally said, "if somebody wants it bad enough they can just take it."

She also said if a cyber crime was bad enough, they would just close down their business and reopen under another name. If you have the same perspective as this business owner, you've got to change your thinking! No matter what you think about your business, I can almost guarantee you it's worth far more than you have ever imagined. Your business isn't just the office building that you own or lease. Your business isn't the sign out front. Your business isn't just your online presence. Your business is the product of an almost infinite number of hours dreaming, working, going through hard times, making the sale, and more. In many ways, it’s worth is also almost infinite.

Vulnerable Because It's Valuable

Your business is vulnerable to attack because it's valuable. The criminals know this. There are aspects of your business that criminals can steal and offer for sale on the dark web. There are other aspects that they know are valuable to YOU and they will exploit that if they can. Their goal is almost always to make money and this reality applies to all businesses of all sizes. In 2019, 74% of businesses were the target of a cyber attack, this trend is forecasted to increase in the coming years.[22] As well, 28% of data breach victims will be small businesses.[23] By maintaining security precautions and following the NIST cybersecurity framework, it is indeed possible to minimize the number of times that you have to deal with these attacks. But every business will at some point deal with it, either because a hacker thinks they found a weakness in your armor or because they want what you and your business have.

What makes a business valuable? It is the result of many pieces coming together, both tangible and intangible. Ultimately, these pieces form something that is greater than the sum of its parts. Many aspects that determine how profitable and valuable a company is can be disrupted by a data breach. Stability and smooth operations, recurring income,

---

[22] ZDNet, 2019, https://www.zdnet.com/article/76-percent-of-us-businesses-have-experienced-a-cyberattack in-the-past-year/
[23] Verizon, 2020, https://www.verizon.com/business/resources/reports/dbir/

loyal customers, and a good reputation for your brand are all things that can be damaged by data breaches. Not only can this impact the profitability of your business today, but breaches can also hurt the overall value of your company going forward. Things like your brand value, cash assets, Personal Identifiable Information (PII) and Personal Health Information (PHI), social media, Google rankings, and the ability to provide for your family and the families of your employees are all at risk.

Unfortunately, when it comes to building something great, it is far harder to build than it is to destroy. You can put a lot of effort into ranking #1 on Google in your area, but an attack can lead to an infected website with malicious code. For this, Google will punish you in their search results, hurting your brand. A social media attack can also damage your reputation and cause a loss of value for your company.

Your business also has cash assets that hackers can target. Even if you can recover them, it may require you to take out high-interest loans in the interim. It could increase insurance costs going forward, even if insurance doesn't cover the full value of the funds. Some assets might not be recoverable at all. Regardless, it means having to waste time and resources recovering your assets from a cyber attack.

On the dark web, stolen social security info, PII, PHI, and credit card information might only bring a few bucks each when sold, but can cost YOU exponentially more than that. The Center for Internet Security estimates that the average PII breach costs companies an average of $158 for each stolen record. This accounts for the cost of potential lawsuits, reduced reputation, cybersecurity protection costs, tracking, and more. When it comes to PHI, that number inflates to an average cost of $358 to the business for the loss of just one record.[24] This is because a person's health information cannot be changed. This information can be used to gain access to settlements, used as information to gain access to other accounts, used to scam victims, and more. If you have the PHI records of 1000 patients stolen, that could mean a cost of at least $358,000 to you. If you have the PII records of 1000 customers stolen, that breach alone could amount to a cost to you of at least $158,000. Keep in mind, it's normal for us to find over 100,000 PHI or PII records when scanning a businesses' network.

Your business is so much more than just what you do. It has so much more value than just a lease and some furniture. Your business is the financial provider for your family, and the families of your employees. That is something you can be proud of but also makes it highly attractive to hackers. They know they can use this value in an attack. This value is something that needs to be protected in our current cybersecurity climate.

---

[24] Center for Internet Security, 2017, https://www.cisecurity.org/blog/data-breaches-in-the-healthcare-sector

After a huge breach, you will need to completely rethink your security apparatus and deal with the long process of recovering stolen assets, changing insurance rates, and rebuilding your brand's value. With all of these things working against a hacked business, the question to ask is, "Will your brand be destroyed by a cyber attack?" Will all that immeasurable time you put into building your business be reduced to nothing? We hope not, and by allowing an expert to optimize your business security practices NOW you can make sure that the answer is a resounding, "No!" when the attack presents itself.

According to Experian, 60% of small businesses who have a data breach will not recover and will go out of business within six months.[25] It is one of my biggest passions in life to help people make their businesses succeed. It's heartbreaking that some companies will close forever — wasting all their potential — because of something they could have prevented. These realities are why I am so passionate about taking the tekRESCUE cybersecurity product to so many people.

Wrapping Up

Our goal in this chapter wasn't to scare you (OK, maybe a little bit) but to make sure you understand how vulnerable every business is in today's climate. We want you to understand the risks and get prepared

---

[25] INC reporting on Experian, 2017, https://www.inc.com/thomas-koulopoulos/the-biggest-risk-to-your business-cant-be-eliminated-heres-how-you-can-survive-i.html

by taking measures to mitigate your risk. Your business is more vulnerable than ever before, but if you start now, you can protect it and lower the risk of disaster to a level that you are comfortable with. Don't put it off any longer. Get moving towards a more secure business today!

About Randy Bryan

Randy Bryan is a cybersecurity expert and founder of tekRESCUE, a Texas based cybersecurity and technology consulting company. He loves leading the tekRESCUE team as they serve the cybersecurity and digital needs of their customers. Their goal is to offer businesses a seamless technology experience that lets them concentrate on their customers instead of their tech. They have won the "Best of Hays" (Hays County, Texas) award for eight years in a row.

When he is not working alongside the team at tekRESCUE, he loves spending time with his wife and family, mountain biking the hills of Central Texas, and working out at the gym. Randy is active in his community, having served on various boards and committees. He also serves as a "North American Brand Ambassador" for OnePlus, collaborating with other OnePlus fans all over the world.

Randy can be reached at

https://bit.ly/ContactRandyBryan

How Less Trust Can Mean More Security

By Nick Stevens

"Don't talk to strangers" is a familiar phrase for many of us. The basic premise of it is a warning: if you don't know a person, then you can't trust them. The stranger may be perfectly nice and wouldn't cause you any harm, but we don't know that. Until you can verify, you proceed with caution.

My goal is to help everyone who reads this chapter walk away with an understanding of how applying this concept of zero trust to cyber security can be a very powerful tool. When you operate your business from a place of caution, the more likely you'll take the necessary measures to secure your organization from cyber threats, as I do for organizations across the United States.

SolarWinds Breach – A Tale of Too Much Trust

In December of 2020, a supply chain attack against the IT software firm Solarwinds, was identified. That cyber attack breached numerous business and US government agencies. Those affected include Microsoft, Cisco, Intel, parts of the Pentagon, the Department of Homeland Security, the US State Department, National Nuclear Security administration, and the US Treasury.[26]

The hack started with the IT management software, Orion, which is sold by a US company called SolarWinds to thousands of companies and government organizations. To successfully complete the hack, SolarWinds itself was infiltrated, and during that breach, the hackers put malicious code into a routine update for the Orion software. Companies worldwide were prompted to update their software for the routine update. This essentially turned the software update into a trojan horse, inviting the hackers' malware into various networks when the Orion software update was installed.[27]

---

[26] Jibilian, Isabella, and Katie Canales "The US is readying sanctions against Russia over the SolarWinds cyber attack. Here's a simple explanation of how the massive hack happened and why it's such a big deal" businessinsider.com, April 15, 2021, https://www.businessinsider.com/solarwinds-hack-explained-government-agencies-cyber-security-2020-12

[27] "2020 United States federal government data breach", https://en.wikipedia.org/wiki/2020_United_States_federal_government_data_breach

The Orion software was considered a trusted software application. It was assumed that Solarwinds was completely secure, and thus the software updates were safe. This trust in SolarWinds meant Orion software had greater access than it likely should have had across the organizations utilizing it. Had these organizations applied the idea of "less trust equals more security," they might have avoided a massive breach.

As introduced earlier, having less trust can be applied as a cyber security and risk mitigation strategy. Formally, this approach is called Zero Trust, which was an idea born in 2010 and first implemented by Google starting in 2011. Zero Trust means that no inherent trust should be given; instead trust is established via the verification of identities (for users) and devices (like computers), at which point, secured access is authorized.[28]

> *"The philosophy behind a zero-trust network assumes that there are attackers both within and outside of the network, so no users or machines should be automatically trusted."*
>
> *-Zero Trust Security (CloudFlare)*[29]

---

[28] Vergadia, Priyanka and Max Saltonstall. "What is zero trust identity security?" cloud.google.com, December 10, 2020, https://cloud.google.com/blog/topics/developers-practitioners/what-zero-trust-identity-security

[29] Zero Trust Security | What's a Zero Trust Network?, Cloudflare.com, https://www.cloudflare.com/learning/security/glossary/what-is-zero-trust/

Zero Trust security has primarily focused on an organization's IT network. Below are both the common components of a Zero Trust security as well as how to have a Zero Trust mindset. These ideas are practical for not only your business, but even for everyday home users.

Components for a Less (or Zero) Trust Security Strategy

1. **Assume Breach**

Approach your organization's cyber security strategy as if you've already been breached. Assume malicious actors are both inside and outside of your network, trying to compromise your software and access your data. People often only think of breaches as something that starts with a hacker in another country or acting from a dimly lit basement. However, reports show that as much as 60% of all breaches are caused by insider threats — this means employees within the company![5] Assuming a breach automatically puts the user on the defensive and helps ensure a thorough approach to security.

2. **Always Verify**

Verify the identity of every person or device before giving access or trust, whether they are in your office or on the other side of the world. Verify, verify, verify.

Multi-factor authentication is one of the most common ways to help verify a person trying to access sensitive resources. If a password is compromised, the second factor of authentication becomes absolutely critical to protecting sensitive data or applications According to Microsoft, users who enable multi-factor authentication (MFA) on their accounts will block 99.9% of automated breach attempts.[30]

3. **Least Privilege (Access Management)**

Only give access to what is needed, nothing more. You don't give your gardener the keys to your car because they don't need access to your car to do their job. Take the same approach to your network, applications, and data. This is especially true of your own employees. If it is not essential to their duties within your company, do not give access.

4. **Access Control (Segmentation)**

This strategy allows for successful implementation of Least Privilege (above). Split up sensitive resources and information into protected silos.

If you've ever been in a secured building, then you've likely seen that every door has some form of access control, like a pin code or card reader. Each access point has a different entry key, and not every employee can access every room.

Continuing with the gardener example, you might put locks on the gate to your backyard and give the

---

[30] Insider Threats Are Becoming More Frequent and More Costly: What Businesses Need to Know Now, idwatchdog.com, https://www.idwatchdog.com/insider-threats-and-data-breaches

gardener access to only those keys. They can access the backyard, but not your car or home, as you've segmented access to each.

5. **Assume all networks are malicious**

Whether in your home, in your corporate office, or using free WiFi in a coffee shop or a hotel, assume there is malicious activity or actors there with you. Similar to the Assume Breach strategy component, you should always be on defense. Implementing the strategies above will significantly mitigate your risk when you encounter a malicious network.

Don't Trust That Network (or WiFi)!

Most of us have become increasingly reliant on our computers, tablets, and smartphones. As a part of that reliance, we desire more and more connectivity to the internet — through our homes, our offices, and everywhere we go. How many places have you been where you've checked if they have free WiFi? Why not, a little WiFi never hurt anyone, right? The problem is that our desire for cheap and easily accessible internet has made cyber attacks, including man-in-the-middle attacks, easier to pull off. This type of attack was well illustrated by an ethical hacker who was only 15, when he presented how easily he could hack a law firm, to a room of legal professionals.

When an unknowing victim using the hacker's free WiFi tried to go to a website — such as their bank website — the hacker could simply redirect a victim's computer to a fake bank website, which could then be used to steal their banking login information.[31] To accomplish this hack, the fifteen-year-old ethical hacker used readily available devices purchased off Amazon for under $100. This equipment allowed him to redirect unsuspecting victims to a malicious website he set up, which wasn't hard since they unknowingly connected to his free, but malicious, WiFi. Many of us are learning to keep an eye out for emails that redirect to phishing websites, but unlike many phishing websites that are used to steal credentials, this attack didn't need a phishing email to kick things off. In fact, one common rule to avoid phishing websites linked in malicious emails is to type in the proper website address yourself, which in this case wouldn't have helped, as the hacker could easily redirect the victim even if the correct web address was manually entered.[32]

So How Do You Protect Yourself?

First, assume all networks are malicious. Remember to be on the defense at all times. When it comes to free WiFi, the easiest option is to avoid it. Most mobile

---

[31] Brinkman, Martin. "Microsoft: 2-factor authentication blocks 99.9% of account attacks effectively" https://www.ghacks.net/, https://www.ghacks.net/2019/08/28/microsoft-2-factor-authentication-blocks-99-9-of-account-attacks-effectively/

[32] Patrice, Joe. "15-Year-Old Hacker Shows Everyone At Tech Show That They're Completely Screwed When It Comes To Security". Abovethelaw.com, August 23, 2018 https://abovethelaw.com/2018/08/15-year-old-hacker-shows-everyone-at-tech-show-that-theyre-completely-screwed-when-it-comes-to-security/

phones can be a personal hotspot, so instead of using free coffee shop WiFi, connect your laptop to your mobile phone's WiFi. If your phone doesn't have this option, or the speeds or your data plan won't work, you do have some other options.

Virtual Private Networks (VPNs) are increasingly common for both personal and business use, especially as remote work becomes increasingly common. Traditionally, VPNs were used to give secure and encrypted access to corporate resources that would otherwise only be available in the workplace. While this is still the case, new options are available that allow you to always have a secure and encrypted VPN wherever you are, both for corporate or personal use.

Don't Trust that Software... or Mobile App!

The SolarWinds Orion breach was a simple example of how software can be a security risk. Whether it is a seemingly trustworthy application from a well-known vendor, or a mobile app on your phone or tablet, you can be at risk. Reportedly, there are thousands of mobile apps available in the Google and Apple stores that are considered cyber threats ranging in severity from obnoxious adware to full-blown malware. In 2017, 75% of all mobile security breaches were through apps, not attacks directly on mobile phone operating systems like Android or iOS.[33]

Some Cyber Hygiene Tips

Be a minimalist when it comes to what software and applications you use. Only download software from trusted, well-vetted companies. Verifying that an app is from a reputable company greatly reduces the chances that the app is dangerous. Also, don't forget to keep your apps up-to-date, as the apps themselves may have exploitable vulnerabilities. Update the applications on your computers and mobile devices. If your business uses mobile devices for work, consider a mobile device management platform that can regulate what apps can be installed and can often segment sensitive company information away from the personal side of mobile devices.

Lastly, if you're looking to really protect yourself, you can enlist an IT professional to deploy and manage application whitelisting and ringfencing. This type of software requires a trained professional but can have huge benefits for security applications and your organization.

---

[33] Britt, Phil. "Mobile & Smartphone Security Threats for 2021". Esecurityplanet.com, February 1, 2021, https://www.esecurityplanet.com/mobile/mobile-security-threats/

Don't Trust That Email!

We've all gotten spam... and lots of it. So much of it that we're kind of numb to the influx, which results in people letting their guard down. In addition to all the spam, phishing emails are getting better every day. As much as 91% of cyber attacks start with a malicious email.[34] Malicious emails have many forms, but some of the most common attacks start with malicious links that redirect you to malware or phishing sites designed to steal your login credentials. Some emails may contain attachments with embedded malware. Other emails use urgency combined with impersonation or spoofing to make it look like the email came from someone you know who needs something done quickly. This can be a request that you buy gift cards for an important client, or a request to the HR team to change direct deposit details.

Protection from Malicious Email

So how can you protect yourself from these spam or phishing emails? First, make sure to always carefully review and verify the sender of each email. This includes checking the actual email address, not just the name shown next to the email address. Hover over

---

[34] Sjouwerman, Stu. "91% of cyberattacks begin with spear phishing email", https://blog.knowbe4.com/, November 29, 2020, https://blog.knowbe4.com/bid/252429/91-of-cyberattacks-begin-with-spear-phishing-email#:~:text=Antony%20Savvas%20at%20Computerworld%20UK,security%20software%20firm%20Trend%20Micro

links to see if they look suspicious and only open attachments from senders you've verified as legitimate.

Second, consider security awareness training for your organization. This allows your employees to learn cyber safety skills through video courses and simulations.

Lastly, consider reaching out to an IT professional so they can assist with configuration of email security platforms that can scan attachments, links and look for tell-tale tell signs that an email is fraudulent. These platforms can add additional benefits by screening outbound emails as well. This assumes that your email has been breached and can help reduce the chance of malicious actors sending spam from your email system.

Applying Zero Trust to the SolarWinds Breach

It's impossible to be 100% certain that specific strategies would have completely prevented the SolarWinds breach. However, based on what we know, it's very likely the breach could have been mitigated. Once the malware was installed, it needed to phone home to let the hackers know it was in. At this point, a Zero Trust approach might have helped, as it would have required least-privilege and access control, controlling what the software could communicate with. The software would only be allowed to communicate externally if it was going to places previously determined to be safe and legitimate. This may have exposed the hackers if unauthorized external communication attempts were seen, or at the very least, prevented the initial phone home by denying communication attempts that weren't previously determined to be necessary.

Additionally, it was found that once the hackers were in the networks, they created new user accounts that mirrored legitimate user accounts. These accounts weren't forced to verify via MFA or other methods to confirm their authenticity.

Finally, the companies employing Orion did not assume their updates were malicious nor did they segment access. Not only did the update happen without pause, but the malware had significant access instead of heavily limited and isolated access. While the SolarWinds breach is, admittedly, an extreme example, it helps illustrate how trust shouldn't be given easily.

In summary, applying the components for a less or zero trust security strategy improves your security posture and reduces the risk to your business or organization. You don't need to be a large company or the US government to start leveraging zero trust. Start with a mindset that your organization might be breached and your data already at risk.

Think about how you can segment the data within your business. Once segmented, you can make sure each person only has access to what they need and nothing more, in line with the idea of least privilege.

Assume all networks are malicious, avoiding the use of free internet when possible and consider methods to encrypt while on all internet connections. Lastly, leverage increasingly common tools like multi-factor authentication to verify everyone before they can access your data. And remember, never trust before you verify.

Get a free copy of our Zero Trust Tips at:
https://www.heroictec.com/zerotrusttips.

About the Author

Nick Stevens grew up in Silicon Valley where he caught both the entrepreneurial spirit and the technology bug. This affinity towards business and technology is also shared with Nick's close friends, many of whom have started, run, and sold successful technology businesses. After graduating from college with a business degree, Nick started his career in technology as an IT support technician helping small businesses primarily in the legal, accounting, construction, and technology industries; manage their computer networks, software and websites.

In 2011, Nick was able to mark off two things on his bucket list, he married the love of his life and co-founded Heroic Technologies, which at the time was a boutique IT consulting firm with a focus on law firms in Silicon Valley. While continuing to hone his technology craft, Nick relocated to Portland, Oregon where he opened the 2nd office for Heroic Technologies. Nick and Heroic Technologies now support and protect business up and down the west coast of the United States. Securing assets and employees spread throughout the Globe. Helping to implement security platforms, policies and programs for small family businesses to international businesses with strict compliance requirements.

Nick loves spending each day balancing technology and people and process, to help ensure his clients can be anywhere, be productive and be secure.

Cybersecurity in 2021

By Robert Medina

Gone are the days of "G-Squad" or break-fix technical support. Hiring a family member or taking on a DIY tech support will no longer do. Installing anti-virus software that you never update or setting reminders to update security patches will only get you in trouble.

The COVID-19 pandemic exposed security holes and process gaps for many businesses, be it health care, retail or the neighborhood insurance agency. The pandemic also served as a differentiator between federal, state or local government agencies – highlighting those that were prepared and exposing those that were not. Earlier this year, the Colonial Pipeline suffered a cyber attack; business files were encrypted, requiring a ransom of over $5 million to recover data.[35] The insurance giant CNA Financial

---

[35] https://www.nytimes.com/2021/05/13/us/politics/biden-colonial-pipeline-

Corporation was also hacked, and it took several weeks to recover from the ransomware attack to the tune of $40 million paid to cyber criminals.[36] And last, but certainly not least, our gecko friend from GEICO couldn't charm his way out of the January-March 2021 data breach that contributed to fraudulent unemployment benefit claims across the US.[37] All of these attacks could have been prevented. If hindsight is 2020, then 2021 was not learning from its mistakes!

The steps and technology tools required to secure an IT environment have drastically changed. Managed Service Providers (MSP) and Managed Security Service Providers (MSSP) are learning, some the hard way, that they need to shore up their technical support stack, preventative measures and processes in response to the tactics of cyber criminals today. They need to know how to prevent system breaches or data theft from happening to themselves and their clients. MSPs are getting a wakeup call as they realize that cyber criminals are more focused and intentional than ever.

The reality is this, security measures have to be successful in preventing every attack while the attackers only have to be successful once. And these

---

ransomware.html#:~:text=WASHINGTON%20%E2%80%94%20The%20operator%20of%20a,Biden's%20efforts%20to%20deter%20future

[36] https://www.bloomberg.com/news/articles/2021-05-20/cna-financial-paid-40-million-in-ransom-after-march-cyberattack?utm_source=url_link&fbclid=IwAR3af13fwTrdLhqAcTCF07hAuQMMrXqULSOCNnrlebBvhBsvA9YfHhr4eVI

[37] https://www.insurancejournal.com/news/national/2021/04/22/610750.htm

attackers are not just focused on nation states, big business or government agencies, but have placed small businesses in their crosshairs, capitalizing on the COVID-19 chaos. Unfortunately, these hackers are forcing small businesses to leverage their cash flow, savings, or borrowed money to pay system and data ransoms. And if owners don't pay, their business might go under anyway.

What is causing changes in the cybersecurity landscape? I believe part of it is a lack of awareness or a passive mindset on the part of business owners, business executives and even technology professionals. They might also lack the understanding of how to align cyber security with their business processes.

Hackers are skilled and adapt well to preventative measures. They are motivated by financial gain and will spend weeks, months, or sometimes years identifying the weaknesses of target systems in order to maximize their impact and financial gain. They hunt for businesses that will pay out. And it's not necessarily big businesses they target but ones that are most vulnerable. Ransomed data, reputational damage, system outages or intellectual property theft are just a few carrots used to get your attention. How do they get you? Social engineering attacks, failed email filtering, improper monitoring of critical systems, phishing, spear phishing and ransomware are the most popular ways they accomplish their goals.

The question is NOT how we stop hackers, but how long it will take to acknowledge the landscape change and adapt accordingly.

Watch Your Step

When in a minefield, you watch your step. Similarly, overstepping or sidestepping could be the difference between success and failure when it comes to securing IT infrastructure. Understanding the negative impact of something missed or misunderstood when securing your IT environment is not just key but necessary in avoiding a cyber-attack.

Naval Officers, Master Chiefs, Senior Chiefs, Chiefs, Airman, Fireman and Sailors on the USS Nimitz Aircraft Carrier, a floating city at sea, walk in sync across the decks of this legendary aircraft carrier to complete a Foreign Object Damage (FOD) Walk-Down. FOD Walk-Downs are routine activities on active aircraft carriers to prevent debris from damaging aircraft engines.

Everyone on an FOD Walk-Down looks for rags, pieces of paper, articles of clothing, nuts, bolts or tools that have been misplaced or caught by wind currents from aircraft operations and blown across the flight deck. If these items are missed or not recovered, they might cause severe damage to aircraft engines and even injury to personnel. One small item overlooked can mean millions of dollars to recover.

The F-14 Tomcat was the fighter jet of choice on the USS Nimitz before they were both decommissioned. The cost for this sophisticated aircraft is approximately $38 million. Boeing estimates that FOD caused an estimated $4 billion in damage to engines – aircraft were taken out of service each year while in active duty because of FOD. When this occurs, resources have to be reallocated, operations are stopped or delayed, reports filed, and staff disciplined.

It cannot be overstated that every step matters during a FOD Walk-Down.

Similarly, business owners, employees, and IT support (MSP/MSSP) must take an "all-hands on deck" approach and work together to walk the "flight deck" of their business or organization. Everyone involved must take an active role in ensuring that all the items that will hinder operations are identified, removed, or replaced so that IT runs smoothly, productivity continues, and organizational success is achieved. You may have invested several thousands or tens of thousands of dollars on your IT, but if even the smallest of items is missed, your business still can suffer. You might have to reallocate resources to resolve the issue, experience delayed or missed projects deadlines due to failed systems, or worse, undergo a complete shutdown of operations because of a successful cyber attack. The only way to prevent this is to build a culture of teamwork, collectively taking one step at a time to identify and remove the processes and procedures that left your business vulnerable to cyber security risks.

Minimize the Casualties

In order to minimize casualties in the cyber risk minefield, all must take a post and be prepared to prevent the attack. Your business must have processes in place to minimize casualties and you and your employees must buy in. I believe there are four pillars of protection encapsulated by a monitoring, altering, and reporting system that must be in place to secure an IT environment.

1. Next Generation Firewall (NGFW) / Edge Security – Protect the outer perimeter of your IT Network, controlling inbound and outbound internet traffic
2. Email Filtering – Scan and filter all in and outbound email communication to prevent phishing, spear phishing and malicious payloads from being executed from within the network
3. Endpoint Security – An endpoint protection platform (EPP) that will include an endpoint detection response (EDR), IoT Control and Workload Protection
4. Breach Prevention Platform (BPP) – Scan and identify the human element of security by combining the components needed to identify, educate, and manage employee vulnerabilities.

The above pillars will need to be reviewed often to ensure that best-of-breed toolsets are applied and in use. Hold frequent meetings with your IT provider — every quarter or no less than twice a year. This will ensure your IT is running on all cylinders as well as aid in keeping IT processes and security top-of-mind.

This chapter is not meant to assist with the details of implementing strategies for cyber risk mitigation, but to make you aware that the cyber risk landscape in 2021 has changed. Your business' cyber security tools might require an adjustment to better mitigate the cyber security risks that we now face.

An oft-quoted bon mot — frequently attributed to Albert Einstein, Benjamin Franklin, or a number of other people who probably never actually said it — is that insanity could be defined as "doing the same thing over and over and expecting different results."

What will you do differently?

For assistance in implementing the above or to speak with a cyber security professional, feel free to contact us by scanning the QR code below.

About the Author

Robert Medina, Founder and CEO of Tier1 Solutions, LLC.

After dropping out of 3 high schools and getting his GED, Robert decided to leave the Little Village neighborhood located in the inner city of Chicago and join the United States Navy. It was at Naval Air Station Miramar, the Top Gun Naval Base Command Center, where the desire for technology and the pursuit of a career in technology began.

After being honorably discharged, Robert landed several technical and leadership roles with companies such as Northern Trust Co, JP Morgan Chase, Bank of America and Merrill Lynch. Robert spent the majority of his career managing the infrastructure for low latency trading environments which included but not limited to, Desktop Engineering, Server and SAN Configuration and Support along with maintaining the upkeep and support of the network infrastructure for several offices throughout the United States. After 16 years of service, Robert ended his career as a Vice

President of Global Operations at Merrill Lynch and decided to leverage the leadership skills learned in the Navy along with the technical skills obtained over the years as an IT Professional and start his own business, hence the birth of Tier1 Solutions LLC in July 2014. Tier1 Solutions LLC is a certified Veteran Owned Small Business with S-Certified Minority status in the Federal System for Award Management (SAM) Database. Tier1 Solutions takes pride in serving the SMB community, local and federal government organizations with IT Services and Solutions with a focus on Cybersecurity Risk Mitigation.

What is the Dollar Value of a Cyber Attack?

By Brett Harrison

In the world of IT and cyber security, things have changed. Gone are the days of downloading a virus onto your computer that is easily removed and cleaned up by your local computer repair shop. Hackers have evolved; they are more sophisticated, and they are running operations designed to steal your data, hold you ransom, and even sell your data to other cyber criminals.

In 2021, all businesses have data that hackers are looking to steal. Depending on the type of business you are in and the size of your business, the amount of data a criminal is interested in varies, but any business that has customer information is susceptible to a hacker who is looking to get their hands on valuable data. The more data you have, the more enticing you are to a hacker and the more time they will spend trying to break into your network to steal your data.

Several months ago, we got a call from a local veterinary office that experienced a ransomware attack. They needed assistance obtaining $25,000 worth of bitcoin to pay the hackers a ransom in the hopes of having their data unencrypted. The veterinary office had no previous relationship with an IT provider as the owner's nephew had gotten the office up and running on a shoestring budget. Beyond that, there was no ongoing IT management or maintenance. Unfortunately, there was also no cyber protections in place. The business did not have cyber insurance, the backup system was a USB external hard drive connected to their server and, while there was basic antivirus installed on the computers, it hadn't been updated in months and was even disabled on several computers.

The business's backup system became encrypted because it was connected to the server via a USB cable. We did inform the business that paying the ransom doesn't guarantee they'll get their data back and perpetuating these criminal activities by paying them is not recommended. But, given the circumstances, paying the ransom was their only option if they needed their data back.

The business elected to pay the ransom and luckily the files did decrypt, although it took several days for the process to complete. While it cost the business

$25,000 to the hackers, the total cost of the incident involved significantly more expense.

Let's consider the cost of all of the things that need to happen when stolen data occurs.

Cost #1: Downtime

After your organization has been hit with a cyber breach, downtime is a common occurrence because the data needed for everyday business operations is inaccessible. Your business activities are forcibly halted until data is restored from a good backup or a ransom is paid and data can be decrypted. A cyber breach disrupts many aspects of a business, but especially daily operations. What does it cost to operate your business each day? Multiply that by the number of days you can't serve clients or have cash flow. The money you're losing can add up quickly.

Cost #2: Financial Loss

In 2019, the average cost of a cyber security breach to a small business was $2.2 million. Damage or theft of assets/data equaled $1 million and disruption of normal business operations accounted for $1.2 million. Hopefully, you have purchased a cyber insurance policy to help mitigate a large portion of these costs, but even with a cyber insurance policy you still may be responsible for a portion of the costs associated with a breach. It is also possible that your insurance won't cover the claim if they determine that the breach occurred due to gross negligence on the part of the insured. Let's take a look at the different ways a financial loss can originate:

- **Direct Loss** - Direct loss is typically fraud directly against the company or an employee of the company, resulting in an immediate loss such as a wire transfer or purchasing of gift cards.
- **Indirect Loss** – These are losses relating to the breach, such as loss of income, opportunity costs, or paying employees who can't work.
- **Ransom and Extortion** – These are payments made to cyber criminals to decrypt data when a business does not have good backups, or are payments made to prevent information from being published on the dark web. The dark web is a place where criminals buy and sell information to use for illegal purposes. Nearly all ransoms and extortions are demanded in Bitcoin as cryptocurrencies are very difficult to track and trace.
- **Remediation Costs** – When a cyber breach occurs, there are several components in determining how it occurred, what information was involved, and what needs to be done to make everyone whole.
    - **Cyber Incident Response Professionals** – When a breach occurs, a team of incident response professionals need to respond to the incident. This is a specialized field and generally is one of the largest costs associated with responding to a data

breach. These professionals will direct and handle the process of dealing with a breach from start to finish.

- **Cyber Forensics Investigation** – An investigation needs to be completed to determine how the hackers infiltrated the network, as well as determine what data was stolen.
- **Fines** – In the US, each state makes its own cyber security laws. Typically, penalties are assessed for compliance violations on a per record basis. The average cost is about $200 per breached record.
- **Credit Monitoring and Notification** – For any exposed records that include Personally Identifiable Information (PII), credit monitoring needs to be provided to the individuals who have had their information stolen. First, however, individuals need to be notified that their information was compromised. Because they may have questions about what this breach means for them, a call center must be established to provide information for those impacted.
- **Legal Fees and Lawsuits** – If other companies or individuals are affected by the cyber breach, there is a good chance lawsuits will ensue in order for the affected parties to recover their losses.

Cost #3: Reputation Loss

Any business that suffers a cyber breach will suffer some form of reputation loss, especially if the data affected becomes public record. However, certain types of businesses will suffer greater reputation loss than others. If a restaurant gets breached and credit card information is stolen, customers may be annoyed and choose not to dine at that restaurant for a period of time. On the other hand, if a financial advisor gets breached, this is a bigger issue since a financial advisor will have much more Personally Identifiable Information, including bank account numbers or social security numbers. In this instance, clients may elect to pull their money out because they don't feel confident in the firm's ability to protect their data. They will likely switch to a new financial advisor that takes cyber security more seriously. Additionally, a financial advisor must be transparent about a cyber incident. The executives of the firm are liable to serve jail time if they do not properly disclose the breach and provide sufficient remediation services.

Cost #4: Information Loss

Does your business have any intellectual property that it relies on to run the business? If that information was gone and not recoverable, would your business be able to continue operations? What if your intellectual property was released to the public and your competitors could learn your "secret sauce"?

Cyber Liability Insurance

As you can see, there are various costs associated with a cyber breach, some of which are hard costs and some of which are soft costs. Many small businesses simply cannot afford the costs of remediating a cyber breach, so having cyber liability insurance is critical. A good cyber liability policy will cover most, if not all, of the hard costs associated with a breach, assuming that you are doing the things necessary to stay compliant with the insurance policy. Making sure that you are compliant with your cyber liability policy should be at the top of your cyber security strategy.

While having adequate cyber insurance is critical for any business, the best option is to work with an IT service provider to keep your business protected from cyber criminals in the first place. While nothing can be done to fully protect your business, steps can be taken to significantly reduce risk and the chance of a breach occurring. At my firm, our number one goal is preventing cyber breaches and keeping our clients' networks secure. We work hard every day to ensure we are doing everything to help our clients navigate the ever-changing cyber security landscape. We all must face the unfortunate reality that we live in a world where cyber criminals are attempting to infiltrate businesses every minute of every day. Staying one step ahead and practicing good cyber security hygiene will ensure that your business doesn't fall victim to cyber criminals. With a cyber breach, you could potentially lose everything you have worked so hard to build.

About the Author

Brett Harrison is the founder and President of Right Click Computer Solutions, a leading Managed IT Services provider based in Bellmore, NY primarily serving the Long Island and NYC area. Brett founded Right Click Computer Solutions in 2011 to help business owners use technology to keep their businesses running efficiently and securely. Previously, Brett owned and operated Brett's Computers, which provided walk-in, onsite and remote computer repair services for individuals. While Brett's Computers was a growing business, Brett saw a larger and more fulfilling opportunity to help small and medium business owners effectively utilize technology and shifted his focus to launching Right Click Computer Solutions.

Brett and his team strive to provide the very best IT and cybersecurity services while forming long lasting partnerships with its clients. Brett takes pride in helping business owners streamline their business by utilizing technology while at the same time educating clients about cybersecurity risks and what can be done to keep businesses safer from cyber criminals.

In his free time, Brett enjoys spending time with his wife Chelsey, traveling, and attending concerts, specifically Dave Matthews Band. He is also an avid Mets and Islanders fan and loves dogs.

If your business has IT needs or is struggling with cyber security, Brett is available to speak with you. To book a short introductory call with Brett, go to http://1x1WithBrett.com.

You can also visit our website at

www.rightclickcomputersolutions.com.

Telltale Signs You Have Been Hacked

By Scott E. Palmquist

For Christopher, it seemed like just another Monday, except email was much lighter than normal. Normally, he would have the usual Monday morning bombardment of new emails waiting for him, most of which were pesky marketing emails. His calendar was booked with meetings all day today, so he was thankful he didn't have to sort through a ton of new emails. After back-to-back-to-back meetings, he felt something was not right. In an early morning meeting, Wendy said she would forward him an email with a proposal. It had been hours and he still had not received the email.

This is one of the many telltale signs you have been hacked.

Most people think bad actors (we're talking hackers here, not Nicolas Cage) immediately do something to reveal you've been hacked. Current research shows hackers have an average dwell time of 45 days[38] from initial access. Christopher was actually hacked on Friday morning, but the hacker saw that Monday was booked with meetings so they didn't start creating rules and sending emails until very early Monday morning. They most likely were hoping Christopher would be too busy to notice or take any action.

Here are the most common telltale signs you've been hacked:

No New Emails for Hours

When your email is hacked, the first thing the hacker will do is create an email rule that moves all new email messages to a different folder other than your inbox. The bad actors then start sending email as you to anyone and everyone in your contact list to try hacking and/or phishing them. Because the email comes from a trusted person, you, this tactic is usually very successful. If your contact replies to the hacker's email, their response will never go into your inbox. It will go to a folder of the hacker's choosing where they will read and answer the emails. As IT cyber security experts helping businesses secure their computers, servers, and networks, we get calls from new clients with this issue all the time. When this happens, it is important to immediately reset your password to a complex password you have never used before. Then

---

[38] Sophos, A defender's view inside a DarkSide ransomware attack, 5/11/2021 - https://news.sophos.com/en-us/2021/05/11/a-defenders-view-inside-a-darkside-ransomware-attack/

review and delete any email rules created by the bad actor, setup MFA (multi-factor authentication), and setup geo blocking so your email can only be accessed from within your geographical area. It is also very important to notify your contacts of the breach so they could act accordingly if they responded to any of the hacked emails sent from "you."

Security Software/Antivirus Shutting Off or Uninstalled

One of the first things a hacker will do when they get access to your device is shut off or uninstall any security tools and/or antivirus. They will also disable notifications. It is important to make sure you monitor the security software and/or anti-virus icon in the system tray to make sure it is active and updated. For businesses, as we do for our clients, it's important you use advanced threat detection security software with EDR (Endpoint Detection and Response) that includes a SOC (Security Operations Center) for monitoring. This combination will ensure your device is protected, secure, and updated by a team of security experts monitoring the software.

Lots of Computer Activity, Unknown Services, and Known Hacker Tools Installed

Hackers have a set of known software and tools they use. A lot of these tools increase CPU, memory, or network usage and can cause random computer shutdowns or restarts. If your computer or network starts to slow down, randomly shuts down, restarts or there is a lot of activity when you are not using it, check the CPU, memory, and network usage of the running processes. It could be your automatic updates running but it could be a tool used by hackers. Also review the services installed or running. Look for any strange or unknown services.

Here are some current tools used by the hacking community: Process Hacker, PC Hunter, Angry IP Scanner, Advanced IP Scanner, Nmap IP Scanner, ARP Scan, Mimikatz, Mimidogz, Mimikittenz, SoftPerfect Network Scanner, NLBrute, Teamviewer, Anydesk. Some of these tools are legitimate software used by IT cyber security professionals, but they should not remain installed on computers used by end-users.

Pop Ups, Toolbars, Redirections, and Passwords Not Working

There is a lot of low-level malware that is more annoying than a severe hacking threat. In any case, malware could be a sign that you are a target and should be taken seriously. Signs of this are: consistent pop-ups every time you open your internet browser or specific applications, toolbars or new icons on your toolbars that you did not add, and being redirected to different websites when you try to go to a specific site i.e. you go to www.google.com but are redirected to www.usethissearchengine.com instead. Another sign one of your accounts has been hacked is that you cannot log in into your online accounts. If you try to log in to an account (i.e. your bank account) and it fails, you need to reset your password ASAP. Hackers will reset your password to lock you out of your account so you cannot log in to stop their activities.

Social Media Accounts

A telltale sign your social media account (i.e. Facebook, Instagram) has been hacked is your friends receiving social media invitations you didn't send. If your friends start contacting you asking why you are inviting them to connect again, you have probably been hacked. It also works the other way. If you receive an invitation to connect with a friend you are already connected with, their account may have been hacked and you should let them know. Other signs include: new posts, replies, likes, or activities you did not do.

Mobile Devices

A lot of the same telltale signs above apply to your mobile device but additional signs include: reaching your data limit faster than normal or seeing your data usage spike to unusually high levels (if you're on an unlimited plan). Keep an eye out for new apps appearing that you didn't install, your phone connecting to unusual websites when you open internet browser apps, or your friends receiving strange text messages you didn't send.

It is not all doom and gloom. You will notice that most of the telltale signs can be handled by being aware and noticing out-of-the-ordinary events. Other signs can be handled by software or regular routines of checking and monitoring.

Steps to Stay Safe, for Personal Usage

Use MFA (multi-factor authentication) every login you can. Most accounts allow you to setup your mobile device to receive a text with a code every time you log in. Reboot your computer daily and be aware of any strange behavior. Always look for the unusual and do not ignore it. Check your antivirus daily: in your system tray where your clock is, drag your antivirus icon and put it right next to the time. Then each time you look at the time, glance at the icon and make sure it is active, updated, and without error. When you see anything unusual, engage an IT professional to scan and clean your computer. We recommend using a local computer store or tech. Be very careful when googling for tech support. There are quite a few hackers who advertise as companies that help clean your computer when what they really do is install their hacking tools.

Steps to Stay Safe, for Business Usage

Here are some current technologies we include for our business clients that you can use as a start for you cyber security checklist:

Employee Training

1. Define your company's security policies, review them will all employees, and have each employee sign off on them. Create a culture of device, network, and data security. Get your team thinking about security and teach them how to respond.
2. All employees should go through a cyber security awareness training program. Regular phishing test emails should be sent to them to see if they fall for the fake phishing scams. End users are the best way for hackers to get into your business.

Make sure your users feel comfortable notifying you they have been tricked. It is an important balance to make sure you enforce your policies but allow for your users to feel comfortable notifying when they've been hacked or tricked.

Use Compliant-Specific Tools

Use advance threat detection anti-virus and a SIEM (Security Information and Event Management) with EDR – Endpoint Detection and Response and SOC (Security Operations Center). This will fulfill some of your compliance needs, if you have them, and give you assurance there are professionals monitoring your devices and networks 24/7.

Consider adding zero trust security to your devices and networking. Zero trust security blocks everything by default and follows a least-privilege model. It will lock down your devices and control what applications can do, how they act, and what communicates over the network.

Design a Disaster Recovery Plan

Always, always have a disaster recovery plan. Assume you will be hacked and/or hit with ransomware. What is your recovery process? How long can you be down? What is your notification process? Who manages the recovery? How much data can you afford to lose and still recover: one day, one week, a month? We protect our clients like we expect them to be hacked so when it happens, we have a plan and are ready to get them back to normal within the timeline they need.

Engage a Cyber Security Professional

We recommend you engage a local IT company who specializes in cyber security for businesses. The risk and liability to your business is too great to have it managed any other way. The cyber landscape and tools are in a constant change and it is the job of the IT cyber security firm, like Computer Support Team, Inc., to adjust the tools needed so your company stays safe.

Contact Scott E. and Computer Support Team for a free strategy call at 818-332-7930 or:

www.yourcst.com/minefield.

About the Author

Scott E. Palmquist helps businesses leverage technology to help their productivity and bottom line while keeping them safe from hackers. Back in the days of DOS he was an At-Home Dad. "It was great to be able to make the choice to stay home with our son." His musician days (as a drummer) were over and he was ready to stay home with his son. To keep his mind, and entrepreneurial spirit, alive, he traded his drum set in for a computer. He spent the next few years helping friends and family with every tech issue and need. Eventually, his wife's employment situation changed and they decided it was her turn to stay home with their son.

Enter Microsoft Certification. After a year of hard work and great hands-on experience, Scott E. had a business. Through referrals, his business grew quickly. He still supports his very first client. In fact, most of Computer Support Team clients have a 18-plus-year history with them.

He states: Computer Support Team's business model puts the risk on us, not on our client. Our mission statement explains it best. Our Mission is to gain mutual trust and respect by providing superior technology consulting and IT security solutions that:

- BUSINESS OWNERS value as helping their bottom line
- EXECUTIVES benefit from productive employees
- END USERS want to refer
- CST TEAM MEMBERS are proud of
- VENDORS want to recommend

Since being featured in his first book EasyPrey, an Amazon #1 best seller released in 2016, Scott E. has been established as the go to expert on Cybersecurity for businesses.

If you would like to reach Scott E. Palmquist, you can do so using one of the methods below:

ScottE@YourCST.com
www.YourCST.com
• www.linkedin.com/in/ScottEPalmquist

Is Your Email Being Hacked?

By Bob Michie

Email is a goldmine for hackers to access your personal data, business files, and other online application logins. Therefore, you should be careful with email security to minimize the damage to your business, intimate secrets, finances, and legal documents. In this chapter, we will identify the signs of hacked emails and the steps to avoid getting hacked. We will also discuss the ways hackers use your emails and a simple method for determining if your Office 365 email system is really secure.

Signs of Hacked Emails

Your email contains much of your business's necessary data. Therefore, you want it safe from hackers and malicious software. However, it can be hard for you to determine whether your email is being hacked or not. Here, we will tell you five signs of hacked emails. If you see any of these signs, you should check the security score of your email using the link found later in this chapter and take necessary security actions.

1. Your password has been changed

A password change is the most prominent sign of hacked email. You will find you cannot sign into your account even after trying the password several times on different devices. If your email is showing an incorrect password this may indicate that someone else has hacked in and changed your password.

You should initiate the password recovery process in this situation. If you have a second backup email, you may be able to quickly recover your password. If not, you should contact your IT service team for help.

2. Unusual Inbox activity

This situation occurs when hackers don't change your password but, instead, they engage in different activities with your email. For example, you might see unusual inbox activity, like emails from a person you don't know. Or emails marked as read when you have not reviewed them, which likely means a hacker is reading your emails.

You can determine if a hacker is indeed using your email by going to your "Sent Emails" folder. If you find any email that you didn't send, it means some fraudster or hacker is using your email account.

Additionally, you often see many spam emails if your email was hacked.

3. Password Reset Emails

If you receive unexpected password reset emails, these could be signs of email hacking. If you did not request a password reset, there is a probability that someone else is trying to do it. But that is not all. A password request link can be malware from hackers trying to extract your credit card info and business data.

Therefore, if you receive any strange password reset emails or verification emails, you should take security steps to protect your email.

4. IP address not matching

Most email services track your IP and show you the login history of devices along with the associated IP addresses. Therefore, if you notice any signs of email hacking like the ones mentioned previously, you should immediately look at your IP address history. If some hacker is using your email, you will get his/her IP address from the list provided by your email service.

If the IP addresses are suspicious and do not match your device address(es), immediate security action can save your essential data.

5. Complaints from friends/family

If any of your colleagues, friends, or family members complain about suspicious emails coming from you, it is a clear sign that someone else is mistreating your emails and engaging in strange activities.

How Hackers Hack Your Emails

There are several ways hackers can hack into your email. Here, we will discuss three of the most common ways your email can be hacked.

1. Someone finds your password

The simplest email hacking case is when one of your colleagues, friends, family members, or anyone other than you finds your password and logs into your account. This case is not too dangerous because these people are not professional hackers and most likely are only doing this for fun. However, sometimes they can blackmail you by extracting your personal data.

2. Ransomware in the cloud

The hacker's most favorite method is to send emails to you or your staff to gain access to your cloud accounts and earn money by blackmailing you. These hackers send security emails or password reset emails with similar names to your service providers such as Microsoft, Gmail, Yahoo, or Hotmail, and urge you to click the link for security verification. These hacker emails demand access to your personal data and files which might seem normal so most people allow access.

Once you or your team members click the link, the hackers can access all your cloud data and encrypt it for financial gain. The real scary thing here is that the cloud access that was granted bypasses ALL security software installed on your local computer.

A video example of this is available at: **https://RANSOMCLOUD.CyberSecurityMinefield.com**

3. Password Cracking

If you do not use a strong password (or 2 Factor Authentication) for email and just use a combination of numerals and alphabet, hackers who are password crackers use a brute force algorithm to easily guess your password and hack your email.

What are brute force algorithms? Brute force algorithms are software that use different combinations of the alphabet and numerals to test your password. If you use a simple password, this algorithm will guess the password in a few iterations. Therefore, we recommend using a strong password for email using a mixture of capital and short alphabet letters, numerals, and special characters, along with two factor authentication.

What should you do if your email is hacked?

Here we will provide you with action steps to take if you find any symptoms of email hacking.

1. Change your password

The first step that you should take is to change your password. However, if you lost access to your accounts, you should instantly contact your IT team, verify your identity, and request a password reset.

Make sure that you use a strong password. We have already discussed that weak passwords are easily hackable via brute force algorithms. Additionally, you should change the password of all the accounts attached to your email. This is because hackers can likely access your other online accounts via your hacked email and might continue to harm you.

2. Enable 2FA authentication

Our digital accounts and emails are a magnet for criminals and hackers worldwide. They can put malicious software in your device and encrypt all your files. However, you can use two-factor authentication, also known as 2FA, MultiFactor Authentication to add an extra level of security to your accounts. It is a crucial step for account security, and we will discuss this step in detail later on.

3. Revoke all app passwords

2FA is very helpful for keeping your email account secure. However, some services that need access to your email cannot use 2FA and use a dedicated App password instead. In this scenario, the email system creates a special, app-specific password for email access authorization. Some hackers enter your account via these apps or even create new app passwords to maintain access to your account, even when you change the password.

So if your email account has been hacked, revoke all app passwords on your account and reregister the services or devices that need access. This is a critical step to restoring the security of your account. Contact your IT team for help if needed.

4. Check for rules added to your email accounts

Hackers are using email rules to forward copies of your email to them so they don't even have to log in to your account to see what is going on. If you change your password, these templates and rules remain in your system and harm your security.

Therefore, we recommend you check the rules added to your email accounts and verify the security. If you are using Office365, be sure to go to **https://SCORE.CyberSecurityMinefield.com** to see (and improve) the security of your Office 365 email accounts.

5. Disable legacy authentication

Email service providers provide you with multiple authentication protocols, including legacy authentication. Legacy authentication refers to the authentication request by older clients that don't use modern authentication. In addition, any client using protocols such as POP3/SMTP/IMAP also falls under legal authentication. The bad part is that the most compromising sign-in attempts from hackers comes from legacy authentication.

The best way to protect your email account from malicious requests is to disable or block the legacy authentication protocol.

Back up your email data

Email is an integral part of any business and many businesses share critical data and files via email. If someone hacks your email and encrypts your data, you will lose all your data because Google, Microsoft, and other email providers only provide a limited backup of your data. Therefore, it is your responsibility to back up your data. I'm not talking about downloading a copy of the data when you remember. This should be an online cloud-to-cloud backup service that backs up your email and cloud data daily.

Effects of Hacked Email Account

Hacked email accounts can badly affect your domain reputation. If your account is being used to send SPAM, service providers detect this and start announcing that your domain is sending inappropriate emails. Poor domain reputation is a considerable issue for owners and affects email deliverability. Many modern systems will block your emails. There is also a probability that your emails show up in recipients' SPAM folders despite being valid emails. If you want to make sure your emails are delivered to your receivers' inboxes, check out **https://MORE.CyberSecurityMinefield.com** for tips on making sure your emails get to their destination inboxes and skip the SPAM folder.

Is your email secure?

Almost 3.9 billion people worldwide use email. Widely helpful in business communication, email can contain many important business files and legal documents. Therefore, you must verify your email security. You can check signs of hacked email in section one of this chapter.

Additionally, you can check your Office 365 email security score NOW by visiting **https://SCORE.CyberSecurityMinefield.com**. You will also receive several recommendations for email security improvement, many of which can be implemented right away.

Bottom Line

In this chapter, we have comprehensively discussed signs of hacked email, hacking techniques, and how to recover your hacked email. There was also discussion about checking your email security and recommendations to improve it. If you need to, use this chapter as a reference you can you come back to frequently if you see signs of suspicious activity in your email.

About the Author

Bob Michie

President, MetroMSP
www.metromsp.com

973-404-0190

Bob Michie is the President and co-founder of MetroMSP. Bob is a member of the US Secret Service Electronic Crimes Task Force, Author of Hassle-Free Computer Support and has been a speaker on

Cyber Security for the Morris County Chamber of commerce and the Morris County BAR association. He is the visionary behind the company's approach to overcoming complex technology challenges faced in today's business environment. Bob is no stranger to thinking outside the box and his creative problem solving skills have enabled him to design industry leading service offerings that mitigate cyber risk while solving business problems.

Bob has over 30 years of experience managing teams and improving processes through the use of technology, business analysis, project management, networking and software development skills.

Cloud Security: Start with Multi-Factor Authentication

By Peter R Zendzian

Ladies and gentlemen, let me tell you a tale, a tale about a time when things were safe. A story of trust and deceit, of incredible gain and profound loss. When the (virtual) cloud was fluffy and white.

There was a time when we used software and services that ran on the internet without a care in the world. Most of these services could be accessed through a web browser like Firefox or Google Chrome, and mobile apps on our cell phones. Microsoft 365®, Google Docs, Apple iCloud, Netflix, Gmail, Dropbox™, Quickbooks®, and Microsoft OneDrive were just a few tools we used. We were able to access all of our information from any device if we had an internet connection. We could edit a file in Google Docs on our home computer and then pick up where we left off when at the office. Coworkers were even able to collaborate on the same document. We trusted our bank records were safe. Email just worked, and life was good.

However, I don't know the name of the business or what trade they conducted. I don't think its essential to this tale anyway. Knowing won't change what happened. Whoever it was changed our carefree relationship with the internet forever.

And this is where our tale really begins.

Technology had inundated our world, advancing at an exponential pace. In this ever more complex and connected world, cloud computing is becoming more and more prevalent. Companies are moving faster and faster away from locally run applications like Microsoft and QuickBooks® to cloud-based solutions.

The jargon and complexity of all our new cloud services hide many of the risks. Some companies are aware of these threats and have taken proactive measures to avoid them. But many do not.

According to LogicMonitoris' "Evolution of IT Research Report" from 2020, cloud adoption accelerated due to the pandemic.

We all remember, but the actual numbers show just how much the cloud exploded:

- The public cloud service market is expected to reach $623.3 billion by 2023 worldwide
- 83% of enterprise workloads were in the cloud by the end of 2020
- 94% of enterprises already used a cloud service
- 30% of all IT budgets were allocated to cloud computing
- Businesses leverage around five different cloud platforms on average
- 50% of businesses spend more than $1.2 million on cloud services annually

The modern cloud solved many problems. Companies were able to pay only for what they used when they used it. There was no more hardware to rent or purchase. The complexity of managing software, resources, or any underlying infrastructure was gone. It was a golden age.

These days, we're not living quite the same story. Many businesses and individuals have fallen prey to cyber attacks. As an IT management company that specializes in cyber security, I do what I can to support and advise businesses on how to stay safe. Companies with sensitive information — like defense contractors, health care clinics, and credit card processors — can learn from the stories I'm about to tell.

A Tale of Fake Identities and Cyber Trickery

Our first cautionary tale happened to a small manufacturing firm. The owners' accounting department was tricked into sending $100K to a fake vendor. What happened was an elaborate scheme to steal the owners' digital identity, impersonating him. The thieves went about tricking the company's staff and hiding all the details from the owners until it was too late.

The scheme took months, but it really snowballed when the accounting department received a legitimate-looking invoice from a spoofed email address. Nothing looked suspicious — the payment request was supported by correspondence history with the vendor.

The thieves were crafty. They were able to communicate as the fake vendor with the company's accounting department, building credibility that was strong enough for the staff to believe that the vendor was genuine.

The accounting department sent the payment, and it was not until several months later that owner identified the irregular expense. But by then, it was too late. The company owners were not able to reverse the payment. And to make matters worse, even though the business had a cyber security insurance policy, this incident was not covered because the staff failed to verify the "vendor's" information.

If this story is not enough to show you how devastating a hack can be, our next story is similar, but with the thieves stealing even more money.

Million-Dollar Emails

A business owner was going about his life like any of us would be. He loved his wife and kids, he had a mortgage, car payments, some good employees... and he worked too much.

One day his life changed. On his drive to work, his cell phone rang. When he answered, all he heard was panic, "IT'S EMPTY!! IT'S EMPTY!! THEY TOOK IT ALL!!!" his bookkeeper repeated over and over.

By the time he was able to calm her down, he had learned his business account had been drained of over $1 million dollars. It was everything to this business.

We know now that the thieves had accessed his email and had vast, intimate knowledge of his life and business activities. They knew exactly how he communicated with his bookkeeper, precisely the words he used in emails to authorize bank transfers.

Even more disturbing, these bad actors had access to the business owner's Outlook calendar and impersonated him in emails with the bookkeeper about the detrimental fund transfers. The hackers were even able to answer questions from the bookkeeper and then delete these emails while the owner was in meetings. His bookkeeper had no idea she was emailing with an impersonator, and the boss never knew about the communications.

In the end, the hackers accessed the business owner's email account, impersonated him, and stole more than $1 million. Sadly, he was never able to recover the money. And with just a few simple steps, it was entirely preventable. Starting with one small thing, one thing that was free and easy to use, he would have saved everything.

In 2020, IBM's "Data Breach Report" showed that the global average cost of a data breach was almost $4 million, with the average breach in the United States costing $8.64 million. Of these attacks, 19% were caused by compromised credentials, followed by 19% caused by cloud misconfigurations and another 16% by third-party software.

So, how can we make sure our sad story of a missing million does not happen to us? That's easy. Let me share the one thing that goes a long way in ensuring our businesses are safer.

Multi-Factor Authentication (MFA)

Whether you have heard about multi-factor authentication or not, this is the single most effective tool you can use to secure many aspects of your business. But uptake might not be easy. Multi-factor authentication can slow down your employees and hamper productivity. Some users even complain, refusing to use it because they think the password "mrwiskers2021" is all they need to keep their data safe. Your staff might even refuse to put work applications on their personal cell phones that would facilitate MFA.

What multi-factor authentication does for your business is add an additional layer of security above and beyond any single password. It requires you use something you have, like your cell phone, to verify that you are really you when logging into your computer or service. It's so simple. Anyone can use a password from anywhere and pretend to be you, but add multi-factor authentication and thieves stop dead in their tracks.

Almost all cloud vendors have multi-factor authentication available in some form or another. Microsoft, Google, and Facebook even have it built into their platforms... but users have to turn it on and configure it.

Just MFA alone would have saved our business owner his $1 million dollars — one small, free tool. And these days, it can reduce a potential threat of attack by almost 20%.

We have learned so much since these events mentioned. We all know our employees are our greatest assets. But the thieves, hackers, and criminals attacking the companies we have worked so hard to build have turned our greatest assets into our businesses' most significant threat.

Our businesses are built on trust. We trust our employees, our clients trust us, and we trust our companies are safe.

Cyber thieves, scammers, and criminals are doing everything they can to abuse this trust. Although these criminals are still out there working as hard as they can to attack, hurt, and steal from businesses, the cloud can be safe these days if we take a few small steps to increase our cyber security. Start by adding multi-factor authentication. Don't become another tragic tale.

About the Author

Peter Zendzian

President, ZZ Servers

Peter Zendzian is President of ZZ Servers, the company he co-founded in 2006.

He leads a strong team of service focused experts adept at designing, building, managing and maintaining secure information technology infrastructures that meet PCI, DFARS, NIST, HIPAA and Sarbanes-Oxley compliance.

A motivated and personable professional, Peter promotes teamwork and a family spirit at ZZ Servers – fostering a can-do attitude that clients trust.

Prior to launching ZZ Servers, Peter spent two decades in the U.S. Navy, retiring as Chief Petty Officer in 2009. There, he held a number of leadership roles spanning technology, training and project management. Peter also served as an Electronics Technician at General Dynamics Information Technology after his naval career.

Peter attended the College of Charleston before earning an Associate of Science degree in Electronics Engineering from Tidewater Community College.

Over the years, Peter has demonstrated a talent for quickly understanding and mastering technology, and he is accustomed to handling highly confidential records and documents – experience which has become core to the ZZ Servers offering.

Peter currently lives in Virginia Beach, Virginia.

Why Your Cybersecurity Insurance Claim Could Be Denied for Gross Negligence

By Dan Tayler

Times have changed. Our world is not what it was, even a couple of years ago. The pandemic has reshaped the way we work and the technology we use. It has also created new opportunities for hackers to take advantage of businesses — unsecure remote desktop protocols (RDP) connections have doubled as businesses scrambled for quick remote access solutions in 2020. This has put many businesses at risk. When it comes to technology for your business, there are few enforced regulations requiring that you have cyber protection such as firewalls, encryption, and antivirus. This is changing. Regardless, if you don't take measures to mitigate risk and a cyber safety incident occurs, your insurance company might deny your claim.

Insurance companies have been around for a long time. Their conditions mitigate risk for a business, and their purpose is to minimize the effects of interruptions to your business. It's easy to understand how a fire or flood will affect your business and how insurance steps in. However, it's not always easy to see how cyber crime can affect you. As cyber crime becomes a bigger problem, insurance companies have started to offer extended coverage. When is the last time you checked with your insurance company to verify the extent of your coverage? Depending on your industry, you probably have a lot more risk than the average policy will cover. Will they pay the ransom in a cyber attack? Will they cover lost revenue and expenses? How about credit monitoring and other charges that you will be on the hook for? Don't assume your insurance will cover all your losses in a cyber attack.

As the owner of a managed service provider (MSP), I am well aware that my business is a high risk target for cyber crime. If hackers compromised my security, there's potential for all of my clients to be attacked as well. In 2019, a Colorado IT company was hacked, and a hundred dental practices were ransomed because of it. Insurance companies are changing their levels of acceptable risk quite often now. You might find your rates rising, or you might not even be insurable any more — especially if you don't adhere to standards such as multi-factor authentication and encryption.

Do you have coverage for the type of cyber crime that you are hit with? The Municipality of Westlake-Gladstone in Manitoba, Canada lost approximately $450,000 in a cyber theft. This was in the form of electronic withdrawals in $9950 increments. This is a huge amount for any business! Once discovered, their IT provider checked and verified that there were no viruses or compromises detected on their network. The finger was then pointed at the credit union they dealt with, but no definitive conclusions were drawn. After ten months, they finally made a public announcement about the theft. With no way to recoup the losses and with issues of vendor transparency, the municipality continues to operate in a deficit. Their insurance has not paid out the claim, even though their insurance company says that all municipalities in the province have extensive coverage when it comes to cyber crime.

Four Ways Hackers Hurt Businesses

What are some of the different methods that cyber criminals use to profit from businesses? One method is breaching businesses' cyber security with phishing attempts. Hackers will send fake messages, prompting staff to click on a malicious link. Once clicked on, the hackers will have a foothold in a business' network. They may take months to assess your business, your profitability, and your backups.

When ready, they will execute their plan to destroy your backups, exfiltrate your data, encrypt your network, and demand a ransom from you. If you choose not to pay, they will publicly release your data, or go after your clients individually for smaller ransoms!

The second way hackers go after businesses is steal credentials to online banking or use fake requests for bank transfers. Stolen online banking credentials may have been the cause of the Gladstone incident. Once they have access to bank accounts, the next step is to transfer monies to another account. Typically, those balances will then go to a third, overseas account. Once this happens, the chances of reversing transactions are extremely low.

The third method is to social engineer your employees. If hackers can compromise your email accounts, it's easy for them to find real invoices sent to your business. They will then replicate them, demanding payment in a different method. An example of this happened last year to a non-profit company called Crop Connect based out of Carman, Manitoba. Through sophisticated fake invoices for a conference held at the Victoria Inn, Winnipeg, hackers were able to convince Crop Connect to wire transfer $200K citing COVID for the payment term changes.

The fourth method is to go after your supply chain. What happens if your data is not exposed by you, but by one of the companies you work with? An example of this could be the IT company you use. If they are at fault, does their insurance company get involved or yours? What if you use online accounting software that gets breached? Will a company like Sage or Quickbooks accept responsibility for your company's losses if your online account is compromised? Or what if your point-of-sale support has remote access into your network and this is the vector hackers use to get in? Looking back on the Gladstone theft, hackers used online banking as their way in, but the municipality says they didn't even use online banking. Was it active but not used, or was there a cyber breach at the credit union's end?

PIPEDA and Cyber Security in Canada

PIPEDA (Personal Information Protection and Electronic Documents Act) is Canada's privacy policy. Did you know that PIPEDA requires a business to report a breach if it is reasonable to believe that there is a real risk of significant harm? Significant harm includes financial loss, identity theft, loss of employment, and business or professional opportunities. Even though reporting has been required since 2018, cyber crime is often kept quiet in Canada. This leads to inaccurate statistics about how much cyber crime is actually happening in the country. The RCMP is creating new cyber crime and fraud reporting systems to make it easier for Canadians to report these crimes.

Hackers know that businesses might try sweeping cyber attacks under the rug if they can. In an effort to press your company harder and pay them, hackers will now steal your data before encrypting it. They will then blackmail you to pay their requested ransom even if you have current backups. Why? Because they will publicly announce the hack and release the stolen data if you don't pay up. This happened to Andrew Agencies, an insurance agency with 18 locations across the Canadian prairies. Andrew Agencies was ransomed for over $1M by the cyber criminal group, Maze. When the company declined to pay the ransom, Maze publicly claimed they had exfiltrated data about customers.

Cyber Security Laws in the US

In May 2021, President Joe Biden signed executive orders related to cybersecurity defense. This was in response to the Colonial pipeline cyber attack that left significant areas of the US without fuel for a week. The order required that federal agencies use multi-factor authentication and encryption on all data within the next six months. This is a welcome step in standardization in an industry that is often dictated by cost to a business rather than by the security and productivity standards needed. Insurance companies will be swift to adhere to these requirements as well (many already do). And, like we're emphasizing in this chapter, even more claims will be denied to businesses that choose to ignore their cyber security.

There is talk about making it illegal to pay ransoms to hackers. The logic behind this is pretty simple: trying to lower the profitability of ransomware. While businesses may still want to pay to get their data back, insurance companies will no longer offer this solution to their clients. Bitcoin is the most favoured payment method for ransoms, as it is more anonymous and difficult to track. However, the cyber criminal group, Darkside, found out the hard way that Bitcoin isn't impossible to track — it looks like the US government may have had a hand in disabling their infrastructure and confiscating some of their funds.

Best Practices for Ensuring a Successful Claim and Mitigating Cyber Security Risk

OK, so things have changed. The wild west days of cyber security are nearing an end. So what cyber safety best practices should your business follow to make sure a claim doesn't get denied?

- Identify and quantify the amount of personal indentifiable information (PII) on your network This includes payment card data, healthcare data, and other PII (this includes SSN/SIN, birthdays, email addresses and phone numbers)
- Create and maintain a Business Continuity Plan
- Encrypt your devices that have PII on them
- Implement next-gen firewalls capable of intrusion protection
- Maintain a managed antivirus that is deployed on your whole network
- Roll out Multi-factor authentication on email and other important methods of data access

- Provide security awareness training for staff
- Perform audits on data access and the ability to remove access from lost/stolen devices
- While you can never be completely immune to cyber crime, it's your responsibility to do your due diligence. Don't let your company be the next cyber crime victim one in the news!

References

https://www.itworldcanada.com/article/forbid-paying-criminals-to-end-ransomware-says-cybersecurity-vendor/436010

https://www.gbainsurance.com/avoiding-cyber-claim-denials

https://www.thegraphicleader.com/news/local-news/cyber-attack-steals-nearly-half-a-million-dollars-from-westlake-gladstone

https://www.rcmp-grc.gc.ca/en/new-cybercrime-and-fraud-reporting-system

https://www.priv.gc.ca/en/privacy-topics/business-privacy/safeguards-and-breaches/privacy-breaches/respond-to-a-privacy-breach-at-your-business/gd_pb_201810/

https://www.zdnet.com/article/ten-disturbing-coronavirus-related-cybercrime-statistics-to-keep-you-awake-tonight/

https://arstechnica.com/information-technology/2021/05/biden-signs-executive-order-to-strengthen-us-cybersecurity/

https://library.educause.edu/~/media/files/library/2017/10/urmiafaq.pdf,Frequently

https://www.ada.org/en/publications/ada-news/2019-archive/december/colorado-ransomware-attack-leaves-100-dental-practices-without-access-to-patient-data

https://www.cbc.ca/news/canada/manitoba/cropconnect-farming-conference-scam-1.5898002

https://www.cbc.ca/news/science/andrew-agencies-knew-for-two-months-1.5404675

https://www.wsj.com/articles/web-site-of-darkside-hacking-group-linked-to-colonial-pipeline-attack-is-down-11621001688

About the Author

Dan Tayler is the owner of Brandon Computers and ITAdvisors in Brandon Manitoba.

With over 20 years experience in the industry, Dan has worked in IT roles for companies such as Convergys, Genesis Hospitality, and Prairie Mountain Health.

In 2012 Dan decided to open his own retail computer repair store, and expanded the business to business side under the name ITAdvisors in 2020. He prides himself in "doing what the customer needs, not what they ask for". Deciding to provide a fully managed service offering that includes cyber security was a natural transition for Mr. Tayler. "Businesses need so much more than a computer guy this day and age. They need a trusted partner to help keep their business safe. The businesses we work with have the same core values as us. It allows us all to be profitable and prosperous and secure".

You can book a free strategy session with Dan at https://1x1.itadvisors.ca

The Importance of Testing Security

By Chris Burns, CISSP

Kevin was out with his family eating dinner on a Saturday night when the call came in. It was the call that changed everything for the small manufacturing company he'd spent the last 25 years building to over $60 million in annual revenue.

"Josh, what do you mean there's a message on every computer?"

Josh responded, "Kevin, I have no idea. I came in and the floor supervisor was panicking and said, 'Come here and look.' All I saw was the message that said our files were encrypted and we can't do anything. We are trying to switch to downtime procedures but all of those were on the server." Kevin was panicking and told his family he had to leave the restaurant immediately.

We got the call from Kevin on the following Monday a little before noon and he was still in a panic. His IT company had been working since Saturday night trying to restore operations. I asked Kevin if they had gone through any disaster recovery or business continuity exercises and his response was a faint, "No."

After a long pause, Kevin added, "We had talked a little about it, but we had this device that our IT company sold us that was supposed to get us be back up and running in the cloud in a few minutes. Then we could restore the onsite files in a few hours."

Kevin continued, "The one thing we never did was test the plan and it turns out we haven't had a good backup in over 70 days. I don't know what we can do at this point because we can't even work."

I told Kevin we would deploy our rapid response team and work with his insurance forensics team to get him back up and running. Three long days later, Kevin's company was back to operational, but the harm was done. The insurance company negotiated the ransom down to $500,000 from $1.5 million, but not all the costs were covered. All told, the costs to the company were more than $2 million in lost revenue, reputation, and lost customers. They survived this cyber attack, but barely.

You may be wondering why I started with a story. It's because that event illustrates the main concern I have with cyber security. The lack of testing in cybersecurity is alarming. Businesses will spend thousands to millions of dollars on the latest firewall or antivirus, or outsource their IT entirely, but they don't have a proper test plan in place. Have you tested your Incident Response Plan or your Disaster Recovery and Business Continuity Plan? Hopefully you have those in place, but testing them is arguably more important than just having them. You can outsource your IT, or you can transfer some risk to an insurance company, but when it comes down to it, the liability is owned by the business and the leadership team.

There are many aspects to cyber security that need to be tested on a routine schedule. Both your disaster recovery and business continuity plans (if you have them) need to be tested at least annually, but quarterly or semi-annually is preferred. Running table-top exercises and scenarios with the leadership team is critical to finding gaps in your plans. I only have this one chapter to talk about testing, so I want to focus on what you can do today to test your cyber security. The two aspects I will focus on are: vulnerability testing and full penetration testing. You want to know that the security you have is working so you don't end up like Kevin.

Vulnerability or Penetration Test?

You've spent a lot of money on the latest firewall, the latest antivirus or next-generation antivirus, a great backup system. Your IT company or internal IT people is telling you that your business is safe from hackers. I hate to break it to you but that's a lie. How do you know all the money you've spent is worth it? Are the measures you've put in place really going to work when needed and actually protect the business and reduce your risk? You need testing that stresses your security in order to find the cracks or gaps that might lead to a security incident or breach. In addition, it's how quickly your systems detect and respond to threats that sets your business apart from your competitors and show how resilient your business is to cyber attacks.

Vulnerability Testing

There are two main avenues to testing security systems. One is a vulnerability assessment. This is a relatively quick test that takes a few minutes to a few hours to complete and should give you an overall view of your network and what vulnerabilities exist. A vulnerability is a weakness that a threat actor (hacker) can exploit to gain unauthorized access to your network or a computer.

Penetration Testing

A penetration test (pen test) takes much longer and usually will stretch into days or weeks, depending on the size of your company. However, it is a more in-depth test. A pen test includes a vulnerability assessment, but it goes much deeper. It looks for ways to actively exploit your network and actually emulates a breach or security incident. This is where a white hat hacker, sometimes called an ethical hacker, will do automated and manual tasks. There are three main types of penetration testing.

1. White box
2. Black box
3. Grey box

A white box test involves sharing full network and system information with the tester, including network maps and credentials. This helps to save time and reduce the overall cost of an engagement. A white box penetration test is useful for simulating a targeted attack on a specific system, utilizing as many attack vectors as possible.

A black box test means that no information is provided to the tester. The pen tester in this instance follows the approach of an unprivileged attacker, from initial access and execution, through to exploitation. This scenario can be seen as the most authentic, demonstrating how an attacker with no inside knowledge would target and compromise an organization. However, this typically makes it the costliest option, too.

A grey box test involves only limited information is shared with the tester. Usually, this takes the form of login credentials and sometimes a computer planted on the network. Grey box testing is useful for helping understand the level of access a privileged user could gain and the potential damage they could cause. Grey box tests strike a balance between depth and efficiency and can be used to simulate either an insider threat or an external attack that has breached the network perimeter.

I typically recommend a grey box test with our prospects and customers because it balances cost and time. We call it an "assumed compromise pen test," which gives us access to a computer on a client's network and some basic user credentials. The focus here is emulating a situation where maybe someone internally has clicked on a phishing email that downloads a small program, giving the pen tester remote access to the computer. From there, my pen tester will try to compromise the network and show you the gaps that exist in your cyber security. Normally, this won't cause mass chaos on your network. However, keep in mind there is a chance that something could happen, so if you have some critical data stored for your business, please make that known when establishing the rules of engagement for the pen test!

There's a lot of crossover between a penetration test and a vulnerability test. Look at the graphic below for the main differences between a vulnerability assessment and a penetration test and where they overlap.

The Five Steps to Testing Your Cybersecurity

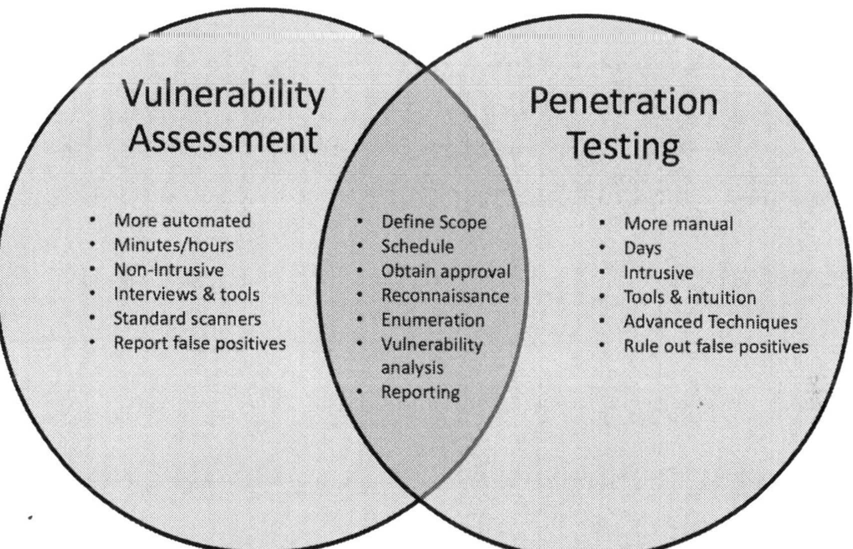

Since there's so much overlap, I'm going to go through the five steps of a penetration test. You should familiarize yourself with the process because you should be doing a penetration test at least once a year. The five steps are:

1. Reconnaissance
2. Enumeration
3. Vulnerability Analysis
4. Execution
5. Document Findings

Reconnaissance

Reconnaissance is passively gathering public information about your company. Here, we would want to find out the format of your email addresses, the executives or key players at the company, the history of the company, and any information we can use to compromise the company.

Enumeration

Enumeration is when the tester is trying to find all your critical assets through a network discovery. If this step was part of a real life hack, the hacker would be after some sort of compromise that exists on your network. One example is someone clicking a phishing email, consequently downloading a payload that had a remote access trojan (RAT). This is the "way in" that gives the hacker control of a computer on your network.

Vulnerability Analysis

Now that we have your network mapped, we run a vulnerability analysis. At this stage, we're looking for low-hanging fruit or any vulnerabilities we can exploit to take over key servers or computers in the network.

Execution

Now that we have access to all your assets and know all the vulnerabilities, we want to actively exploit what we've found through the execution phase. This can either be very loud or quiet. An attacker usually wants to be somewhat quiet, so they don't set off alarms. If your security doesn't have good detection for these threats, you will never know that someone is just moving around your network and stealing things.

Document Findings

Now that we've compromised your network, or maybe we haven't completely, we have to document the findings. This is the report you will see with the results of either a vulnerability assessment or a penetration test. The difference between the two is that the first only shows where your systems are weak, while the second also shows what happened when those vulnerabilities were actually tested. Maybe the tester called your office and socially engineered a password from an employee. Or maybe the tester was able to successful phish one of your executives to gain access to your financial records. A good report will highlight what was found and provide a rating of the severity. You will also get the results of what was actually exploited during the pen test. Finally, there should be a section that has recommendations, in order of severity, for what your organization should address first and how quickly that should be done.

Conclusion

I really want to emphasize how important the system testing is for your business; cyber security is critical. So far in 2021, we've had a SolarWinds supply chain that infiltrated some of the largest governments and corporations in the world. Microsoft Exchange Server vulnerabilities were so easy to exploit — thousands of networks were hacked because of this. The Colonial pipeline that supplies 45% of the oil to the eastern US was down because of a ransomware attack. It doesn't have to be this way. You can't be 100% risk free from a cyber attack, but by leveraging the testing I talked about and fixing vulnerabilities as fast as possible, you can significantly reduce your risk and give your business a competitive advantage over the ones who don't address their cyber security.

One of my passions, and the mission of my business, is helping as many companies as we can avoid being an easy target for these bully-like cyber attacks. I'd love to have a conversation with you about how you're testing your cyber security today. I challenge you to at least start somewhere. In a simple test that takes less than 30 minutes to run, we can test your cyber security and emulate what an attacker could do through. It's 30 minutes that could change your business forever.

Please visit https://techiegurus.com/testmysecurity and fill out the form. One of my team members will contact you and schedule a call. Just remember, what gets tested gets improved, and it's time we all test our cyber security the right way. Happy hunting.

About the Author

Chris Burns started Techie Gurus in 2008 to address a gap he saw in the IT industry between enterprises and small and medium businesses. He saw that too many small and medium businesses struggling with subpar IT and cybersecurity. Thirteen years later Techie Gurus has transformed into a premier cybersecurity focused IT provider for small and medium businesses in Metro Detroit and throughout the United States.

Chris Burns has over 20 years of experience in the Information Technology industry with consulting small and medium businesses, Fortune 100 enterprises, and government agencies. His thirst for knowledge has led to over 55 IT industry recognized certifications including the coveted CISSP (Certified Information Systems Security Professional). Chris has been a featured speaker, graced the cover of MSP Magazine twice, featured in Podcasts, self-published two books, and has been quoted in numerous online publications.

How To Not Lose Everything

By Stew Lambert

The absolute best way to prevent your business from losing everything to a cyber attack is manage your cyber risk successfully, by developing, building, and maintaining a layered defense. To create a successful defense, follow these three principal rules of security: protection, detection, and response.

The easiest way to understand these security principals and how they fit together is to use an example that most of us are familiar with — our own homes. We protect our homes because they contain the things that are most valuable to us such as our families, our possessions, and family heirlooms. We keep our homes safe by installing fences, doors, and locks to keep intruders and thieves from entering.

However, these safety measures only protect if an intruder cannot defeat them. If an intruder is able to open the gate on your fence and pick the lock on your front door, they now have free reign inside your home. Once the thief has entered your home, the scariest part is whether or not you know they are there. You could be in your bedroom watching TV and there could be a threat roaming through your house, but you are unaware the intruder is inside or know how to respond.

A good detection system is invaluable for managing your security risks at home. If the protection principle has been defeated, you need to be alerted that an unwanted person is inside your home. This is where an alarm system is used to detect intruders. Once the intruder has been detected, you then can move to the next phase: how you respond.

The response principle is usually where security systems tend to fail. People do not adequately plan for various types of threats because they never think it is going to happen to them. Or they don't want to think about it happening to them. Do you have a plan if an intruder entered your own home? You should have several response plans in place to shore up your security risks. Does the alarm company call the police for you? Do you have means to physically protect yourself in the event you come face to face with your unwanted house guest? Should you leave your home and let the police handle it? Is there an additional safe for your family heirlooms? Do you have backups of all your family financial documents?

Who do you call if your defenses have been breached? Are you properly insured if your valuables are taken?

Now that I have explained the principals of security, let's apply them to your cyber risk.

Protection

The best way to manage your cyber risk is to build a layered defense and reduce your attack surface. The start of a successful layered defense begins with perimeter security, this means a next-generation firewall that is properly configured and managed. This type of firewall will inspect the network traffic moving in an out of your organization, searching for hackers, ransomware, and other security anomalies.

One of the biggest attack vectors in cyber security is email. It is estimated that 91% of cyber attacks start with compromised email accounts or ransomware entering your organization via attachments or bad links.[39] A good email security provider can be well worth their weight in gold. Building on our layered defense, the next step is selecting proper endpoint protection software. When I started in the industry 20 plus years ago, the importance of antivirus software was not like it is today. Previous generations of

---

[39] https://www2.deloitte.com/my/en/pages/risk/articles/91-percent-of-all-cyber-attacks-begin-with-a-phishing-email-to-an-unexpected-victim.html

antivirus software were signature based. This means that the virus needed to be discovered by the virus companies, which then created a signature that was passed down to your software and files were checked against known signatures. The attack vector has now changed; therefore, the endpoint protection software needs to change. The latest endpoint protection software is behavioral-based versus signature-based. It checks to see what a file is doing. For example, you could download a Word or a PDF document that will look clean to a signature-based endpoint protection but will actually reach out to the internet, download and introduce a malicious payload onto your machine. The latest generation of endpoint protection will notice that a Word document is not supposed to behave in this manner, so it will block that behavior before damage is caused.

There are many more products that can be added to the protection security principle, but the last line of defense is always your users. If your people have not been trained properly and or don't have security top-of-mind, all of your protections could be for naught. End-user training is essential in your organization and happen at least monthly. Your employees should learn how to identify a problematic email or if someone has access to files that they should not. Employee awareness can save your business. We must be diligent all the time —hackers only have to gain access to your network once to cause irreparable harm to your business, your reputation, and finances.

Detection

Now that you've set up the protection principle, how do you detect if there is a bad actor inside your environment? There is one easy answer. Someone must be watching and monitoring your environments. This is done by using a security operations center. These individuals are trained to watch for anomalies and indicators of compromise. They can verify anomalies which may not be noticed by your users. Implementing a security operation center can be expensive, so if you don't have the budget, I suggest looking for a reputable company like Lambert Technology Solutions to help monitor your cyber environment.

Response

The third principle of security? You need to come up with an effective incident response plan. A plan that includes multiple strategies in order to respond to different types of attacks. The key to a good plan is containing and minimizing the effects of the attack. For example, if you were in a ransomware attack, you will need to remove the infected device from the network and quarantine devices to interrupt the spread of ransomware. Next evaluate the damage that has been done, reverse its effects, or deploy a plan to restore the affected systems back into production.

Remember, you should work with your insurance company to determine what needs to happen in response to certain types of attacks. Many times, insurance companies will deploy forensic teams to analyze the attack. The forensic teams will often want to maintain the integrity of the infected systems in order to determine the root cause of the attack. In these cases, you will need the hardware to restore your data from your backup or return operational systems to working mode while maintaining the integrity of the infected systems.

The plans you develop will need testing and evaluation. At minimum, test on a semiannual basis. It has been said that during an emergency, you always fall back to your minimum level of training so make sure your team is thoroughly trained for these scenarios. Maintain both a hard copy and electronic copy of your incident response plan in the event the internet or network is down. The plan should include the incident response team's contact information, as well as the contact information for your insurance company, telecom company, and any third-party technology providers. The plan will ensure that recovery from a cyber attack can happen as quickly as possible.

The final element in your response plan must include two items: A disaster recovery plan, which includes image-based backups, and a cyber insurance plan. These two items can save your bacon after a cyber attack. An imaged-base backup takes a complete snapshot of the PC or server at the time of backup. The advantage to this type of backup is it can allow for the complete restoration of a PC or server without the need to completely rebuild it, saving a tremendous amount of time when restoring systems back into production.

A perfect example of this is when a client experienced a ransomware event several years ago. The accounting person received an email from one of their vendors. The invoice attached came as a Word document. Invoices were normally sent as PDF documents. The accounting person opened the document which released the ransomware into their system. After receiving an alert from the accounting staff, we pulled the infected machine off the network, stopping the ransomware from infecting further machines. We then dispatched a technician to the location and realized the server had been compromised as well and their files were being encrypted. At that point in time, we took the server offline and virtualized the server from its last backup which was less than an hour before the incident. The rest of the company was able to continue working while we investigated the ransomware incident. We decided to format the hard drives of the server and restore the backup to that server during off hours.

Everything was back to normal the next day. Time is money and restoring systems as quickly as possible is an urgent priority.

How long could your business afford to be down?

A Note About Cyber Insurance

Within the past couple of years, cyber insurance has become more scrutinized by the insurance companies. In the past, cyber insurance was a simple add-on to a business policy. With the increase in cyber attacks and ransomware, insurance companies have had to pay out large sums of money. Many of my clients now have to fill out applications with new cyber security conditions that can result in out-of- pocket costs if not strictly followed. Additionally, a colleague in the insurance industry stated he is seeing cyber insurance premiums increase by 50% this year.

The best way to combat rising insurance premiums and prevent your business from losing everything is to establish and document a layered cyber defense. Stay protected. Stay productive. Stay profitable.

About the Author

Stew Lambert has been in the IT industry for 25 years. He spent most of his career in the enterprise space working with Fortune 100 companies and government agencies. In 2014, Stew left the corporate world to start Lambert Technology Solutions to bring enterprise security and efficiencies to small businesses.

The goals of Lambert Technology Solutions are to keep clients Protected, Productive, and Profitable. When not behind the keyboard, Stew enjoys the outdoors with his wife and two children.

What is Your Plan for When You Get Hacked?

By Justin Colantonio

Case Study One: Having A Plan, Being Prepared

This is going to be your week. You arrive at the office bright and early on Monday morning to get a jump start. You sit down at your desk, take a sip of your still piping-hot coffee... and your phone suddenly rings. It's the CTO. You think to yourself, it's odd for the CTO to be calling this early on a Monday morning. You pick up the phone and the CTO explains that the office has been hacked over the weekend. Your drop your coffee mug and it shatters all over the floor. You feel like your stomach is shriveling up into your chest.

As a business owner myself, there are not many things that scare me in quite the same way as a cyber breach. The only other thing that horrifies me more is picking up the phone and the police telling me something awful has happened to a loved one.

You have worked so hard to grow your business into a successful one; you've put in nights and weekends and time away from your family to build it to such heights, then in a flash, all your years of work are jeopardized by someone breaking into your network.

Once the coffee is cleaned up and your mug shards are in the trash, you try and collect yourself. You gather your thoughts and ask senior management to head into the conference room. Once everyone arrives, you attempt to determine what happened. Your CTO explains that, over the weekend, a ransomware payload hit and spawned over the network.

You, as the CEO, respond and ask, "How bad is it?" Your colleagues respond, "Very bad. All the critical business files have been hit."

You ask, "What about our backups; we can restore them, right?"

They explain that those have been hit, too, and your stomach is tied further into knots.

"What about our offsite solution?" you ask.

The response is dire, "That is an option, but we are uncertain how long it will take to restore — it could be a couple of days to download all the data, and there are no guarantees that it has not been compromised either."

Everyone is thinking, So now what do we do?

A rush of scenarios starts going through your mind. Who do we call? Do we pay the ransom? Can we even pay the ransom?

Many of the entities that hack businesses are considered terroristic in nature here in the United States, and paying them is illegal.

The ransom is currently three Bitcoins which is about $150,000 at this point in time.

What is Bitcoin?

Bitcoin is a type of blockchain currency that many hackers ask for their ransoms. The main reason for this is that, once paid, it is untraceable. Now, paying a ransom is not considered a safe option, as you are never sure if the hackers will give back the data back once payment is received.

Luckily, you purchased some cyber liability insurance. So hopefully some of these repair costs will be covered. Since we opted not to pay the ransom, we need to develop a plan on who we need to call.

Steps To Take When A Breach Occurs

When a breach or hack occurs, there are typically a few key players that you need to contact. The first is your insurance company and agent. You need to file a claim and get the ball rolling towards financial damage recovery.

Next is a forensic IT expert. This person is responsible for determining where the breach occurred and if it is still an active threat. They also will have tools that could possibly decrypt your ransomed data files.

You will also need to reach out to your accountant, lawyer, and marketing/PR firm.

Your CPA will help you with accounting issues while your system is down, and if all your data is lost, then they can help start re-building the books.

Your attorney will advise you on what legal ramifications the business is going to face. In many states, there are regulations that need to be addressed, especially if you have personal health information (PHI) or personally identifiable information (PII) data stored.

In many cases, if PHI or PII data was breached, there are laws that require businesses to provide credit monitoring for the people affected. You will have to notify all parties that their personal information has potentially been compromised. Your PR firm will try to keep your reputation intact.

When it comes to a small business, an attack or breach could be the end. For 60% of small businesses, a cyber breach results in failure within six months of a successful hack. The business impact or revenue loss is just too great to overcome.[40]

Now back to the conference room. Luckily, it turns out the IT firm you engaged was able to restore your data from your offsite backup in a reasonable amount of time — it was more of a nuisance than a total loss. However, that is not always the case.

Make Sure You Have an Incident Response Plan

What the company should have had was an incident response plan. Keep in mind, even with this plan, you will still have that feeling of uneasiness. But instead of having to figure out what to do on the fly, you already have a plan to respond to this type of situation.

Here are a few simple steps that go into creating these plans:

1. Address which stakeholders will be involved in the recovery process.
2. Develop a plan of priorities: which systems are considered most critical? Determine what can be done to minimize a breach of the most important data.
3. If a breach was to occur, what are the communication processes that need to occur?

---

[40] https://cybersecurityventures.com/60-percent-of-small-companies-close-within-6-months-of-being-hacked

4. Hire and engage an IT firm to be your incident response IT team; they will be prepared to attack the problem head-on as they already have a relationship with your business. In contrast, the insurance firm might assign someone to you and you will have to go over your systems and the attack from square one.

5. Review your plan annually (or more often) so it is always relevant. Reviewing your plan regularly allows you to identify and fix weaknesses in your plan. You should also test it on an ongoing basis.

Case Study Two: Behind the Ball

But what if your business was not so lucky and didn't have a response plan in place? Let's look at a slightly smaller business, whose IT director, Steve, is not as on top of cybersecurity concerns as those in our first case study.

Steve is great with the end users and responsive at a reasonable rate, but it sometimes feels like the industry has outpaced him. You, as the CEO, have even found yourself losing sleep at night, wondering how your business will handle a cyber attack. There have even been some outside vendors requesting to do penetration testing and evaluate the company's risks, but it feels like overstepping Steve, and no one quite agrees on the best move.

And then it happens... the CFO's email is compromised. No one knows when it started, but fraudulent wire transfers have been made, and vendors are pointing the finger at your company. There have already been threats of litigation. Your phone is ringing off the hook, and you are scared to read all of the emails coming in, written in all caps and with a lot of exclamation marks!

Steve changes the passwords and begins the process of setting up two-factor authentication, but what about the damage that has already been done? This is what we in the industry refer to as "reactive" practices. The hack has occurred, so steps are implemented to stop the bleeding and try and prevent further phishing emails going out.

In a management meeting, it is decided that a third party cybersecurity firm is brought in to dig through what actually happened, when it happened, and what else can be done to ensure something like this never happens again. After the experts are onsite — digging through logs, reviewing emails chains, and interviewing the CFO — it is determined that he clicked on a fraudulent reset password link, a classic phishing scam.

Once the bad guys had the CFO's email credentials, they laid low for a month or so and monitored who the CFO dealt with and what kinds of money was moved around. They waited for an opportune time to strike and made off with about $200,000 in phony wire transfers. By the time the banks were contacted, the receiving accounts no longer existed. To add insult to injury, the amount wasn't large enough for the bank to dig further.

But for your company, $200,000 of your vendors' money, those partners who trusted you, this is catastrophic. Yes sure, insurance kicks in and covers the losses, but trust is not so easily restored. Eventually, the fingers point to leadership, and not necessarily the IT director. If concerns were valid, why was there no push to protect the company, or to innovate?

Training the staff, plugging security holes and budgeting for ongoing cybersecurity protection is not money that can be plucked out of thin air. These measures should be evaluated more often than once a year: quarterly snapshots of where the organization stands, what is on the horizon, and what your long-term planning looks like are crucial for safeguarding against hacking threats.

What you are losing sleep over today could be much, much worse when reality comes crashing down all of a sudden and you are unprepared.

Case Study Three

Let's refer back to your company from the first case study. A year has passed, and all has been quiet in terms of threats. But you have not been resting on your laurels. An outside IT firm specializing in cyber security was engaged shortly after the ransomware attack. Not only are antivirus alerts being monitored through an external portal, but the business is protected from the outside as well. A managed detection and response system is in place that monitors every endpoint for malicious activity.

In addition, every application used on the computers has to be whitelisted before it can be launched, and there is data on this service. The CTO receives reports of blocked programs and it is shocking to everyone how many things were probably slipping through the cracks before this service was in place.

But as Murphy 's Law dictates, one day things hit the fan. But this time, it plays out a bit differently. You do not get a hurried phone call telling you about the breach. Your CTO knocks on the door, sits down, and asks you how your Monday is going. Not too bad really... but what is going on?

Well, it seems that Phil in accounting opened what he thought was just a PDF document, but there was a macro embedded in it. "Did it hit the data drives?" you ask. You can feel your coffee cup trembling in your hands. The CTO smiles, nope.

But what protected us this time? Well, it seems a mixture of factors kept enough of a buffer for the cyber security folks to act. A Priority 1 Alert was triggered as soon as the payload hit Phil's PC. Sure, his PC will have to be wiped, but because the servers are on their own subnet and protected on the firewall, this is not the catastrophe event it could have been. Layers of tools: antivirus, antimalware, cyber security monitoring, application locking, and an engaged incident response team all acted together as pieces of a puzzle.

When attacks are stopped in their tracks, it is still important to convene with management and employees of all levels and ask, “What can we learn from this?” But a learning experience is much easier to handle than a full-on breached data server. There are no calls to insurance companies to make. No relationships with vendors or clients to mend. This is how business and IT are supposed to intermingled.

Key Takeaways: The Plan is to Plan and then Plan Some More

Your IT should work for you but more or less be invisible half of the time. You expect the brakes on your car and your smoke detectors at home to work. IT and cyber security are similar. But this infrastructure does not happen overnight. Multiple layers of protection and having a plan for the inevitable are crucial. Below is a short list for combatting cyber security risks. Together these can prepare you for the inevitable cyber attack. With these measures in place, you will be ready and can respond accordingly.

- Antivirus, antimalware, end point detection and response software
- Firewall with security services
- Spam filtering and two-factor authentication

- Complex passwords with a regular change cycle
- Image-based backup, encrypted with no passwords found elsewhere on the network
- Offsite backup
- Application whitelisting
- Quarterly business reviews, putting in writing your Recovery Time Objective (RTO)
- Partnering internally or externally with cyber security experts who monitor outside the network looking in
- Creating Disaster Recovery (DR) run book that outlines the steps and roles of individuals inside and outside the organization
- Designing an Incident Response Plan

If a business takes these simple steps and puts in the time and effort to protect themselves, a cyber attack becomes an event that you respond quickly and calmly to instead of with panic. Don't be another statistic, but be a champion of IT security.

About the Author

Justin Colantonio

http://www.thetechresource.com

Justin Colantonio is the Managing Partner of Total Technology Resources and one of the founding members of the firm. Born and raised in Northeast Philadelphia, he came of age right as the Internet was starting to take off. Even as a youth, he always had an interest in technology, so much so that he won an award for technology in grammar school. He continued his IT education at LaSalle University, graduating with dual degrees in Accounting and Management Information Systems.

After college, he tried accounting as a career but quickly realized that was not going to be his long-term plan. He then delved into IT. He took a position as an adjunct professor at CHI Institute teaching server management courses. During that same time, he was hired by the City of Philadelphia as a consultant to help implement a new 911 system. Justin spent 2 years there helping the internal IT team complete a large-scale project , seeing it through until installation.

Once the consulting engagement was over in 2004, he had an interest in starting a business. He discussed this venture with a longtime friend and Total Technology Resources was born. Over the past 17 years, Justin and his business Partner Jim have grown their firm into a thriving Managed Service Provider. He is now responsible for the company's vision and direction. He oversees his Executive Management team and has recently developed their new cybersecurity program. Justin currently lives in Haddon Heights NJ with his wife Kate and his two young children.

Is Your Exchange Server the Weakest Link in Your Network?

By Jerry Swartz

For years, the standard for enterprise email was Microsoft® Exchange servers. A huge section of businesses relied on those types of on-premise servers to handle all their emails and calendars for their employees. These servers could be replicated at other satellite offices and many IT people specialized in supporting only them.

As familiar as your on-premise email server feels, I believe the reign of on-premises exchange servers has run its course. In very recent history, several major cyber attacks have made the headlines that involve hacks of on-premise email servers, showing that on-premises servers are an easy target.

SolarWinds® Orion Hack

On December 31, 2020, Microsoft said Russian hackers viewed some of the software company's source code but the hackers were unable to modify it or get into Microsoft's products and services. While Microsoft did not elaborate on what code was accessed, rumors started to circulate. This hack became known as the SolarWinds Orion hack. White House Deputy National Security Advisor, Anne Neuberger, said on February 17, 2021, that the federal review into the SolarWinds hack was in the early stages and will likely take several months to complete. Neuberger said the attack, which compromised "nine federal agencies and about 100 private companies," was launched from inside the United States. On February 18, 2021, Microsoft revealed that the hackers studied small portions of Microsoft's source code, including Azure components (subsets of service, security, identity), Intune, and Exchange.

This was very disconcerting since the hackers had already put the public at a disadvantage for 45 days since the official announcement. Exchange is an integral part of many organizations so, at that point, vendors started reaching out to IT security professionals about moving their on-premise devices to cloud-based services.

On March 2, 2021, Microsoft detected multiple zero-day exploits (vulnerable access points) being used to attack on-premise versions of the Microsoft Exchange

Server. Over the next few days, over 30,000 organizations in the US were attacked. Hackers used several Exchange vulnerabilities to gain access to email accounts and install web shell malware, giving themselves ongoing administrative access to the victims' servers. On the same day, Microsoft announced they suspected the attacks were carried out by a previously unidentified Chinese hacking group they dubbed "Hafnium." Those cyber criminals were using Exchange server vulnerabilities so their botnets could steal processing power. The reason? Using webshells for cryptocurrency mining.

In response, Microsoft quickly released updates addressing Exchange Server versions 2010, 2013, 2016, and 2019. Organizations around the globe frantically started patching their systems. Unfortunately, there were still many security vulnerabilities that the cyber criminals were exploiting. As if things weren't already like a sci-fi movie, the US Federal Bureau of Investigation (FBI) deleted webshells on Hafnium-compromised Exchange Server installations across the country on March 31 and sent notices to victim organizations. After it was found that some webshells still existed after the FBI scan, they used those existing webshells to, in a way, self-desctruct — delete them by sending a command through them. You could say they hijacked the hijackers.

Good News For Cloud Server Users

Companies using Microsoft Exchange online had it much easier, having avoided much of the SolarWinds Orion hack. They have continued to go about their business, unbothered by the scary news that kept coming in. This is because their cloud servers are protected and patched on a regular schedule and watched over by teams of cyber security experts at Microsoft. Each time a new Exchange vulnerability is discovered, it has come with reassuring news for those already in the cloud: it does not apply to Exchange online. During the SolarWinds hack, we were completely booked with migrations — things were looking good for our clients and we felt they had dodged a bullet by being proactive. They — and us — were thankful.

The Colonial Pipeline Attack

You might have heard about the May 6, 2021, Colonial Pipeline cyber attack, either in the news or in other chapters of this book. This attack, credited to hackers, DarkSide, involving ransomware: 100GB of data was stolen, causing Colonial Pipeline to shut down their IT systems and temporarily pause production on a majority of their pipelines.

In response, Colonial Pipeline paid $4.4 million to the DarkSide hacking group on May 7th to decrypt their infrastructure. On May 8th, Colonial Pipeline, along with US government organizations and US companies affected took their hacked systems offline. May 9th: Colonial Pipeline gave an update on their investigation into the attack and on the status of their pipeline operations. On May 10th, the FBI issues a statement confirming DarkSide is responsible for the hack.

DarkSide is a criminal group with origins in Russia. A forensic report of the Colonial Pipeline noted that the "most likely culprit" within the company's IT infrastructure was the vulnerable Microsoft® Exchange services, as noted by New York Times reporter Nicole Perlroth, though there were several other issues that researchers characterized as an overall "lack of cybersecurity sophistication." The Cybersecurity and Infrastructure Security Agency warned pipeline operators about potential ransomware attacks in 2020 and offered several potential mitigation strategies. It appears that these strategies were ignored or possibly just never implemented.

Keep Up With Your Security Updates

If you still use an on-premise Exchange server, it is vital that you keep up with Microsoft's CUs and Sus — Cumulative Updates and Security Updates. CUs are generally released quarterly with resolutions to feature problems. SUs are released when security issues are found and fixed. Microsoft® has found that many companies are not keeping up with updates, and, therefore are not on supported CU versions. This means they don't have the newest security patches – extending the time their servers remain vulnerable.

We are often asked by people why larger organizations' internal IT teams don't keep up with every single recommended protection tactic. The answer often comes down to resources and priorities. Security is vital, but so are maintenance, development, and modernization projects. Also, many companies don't have chief information security officer (CISO) or at minimum, a certified information systems security professional (CISSP) who is responsible for making sure the company uses the best security techniques and practices. However, the March and April 2020 attacks make it clear that companies wanting to keep their Exchange servers on-premises need to maintain constant vigilance, not only with continuous updates and security patching, but also monitoring for nefarious intruders. What do you need to do to keep your on-premises exchange server safe?

1. Buy a certificate every two years
2. Engage cumulative updates
3. Perform security audits regularly
4. Install server monitoring
5. Install firewalls on port 25 of your local network
6. Purchase new equipment/software at every end-of-life

Unfortunately, cyber criminals are not going to go away. They will continue to test the defenses of on-premises servers. As cyber security professionals, we highly suggest it is time for your business to migrate your on-premises server to the cloud. The SolarWinds and Colonial Pipeline cyber attacks make it clear that companies wanting to keep their Exchange servers on-premises have to maintain higher levels of vigilance, not only with continuous updates and security patching, but also with monitoring for nefarious intruders. Cyber security is not a one-time thing to "set and forget." To keep global cyber threats from harming your company, it takes audits and constant reports by security-oriented professionals with CISSPs on staff.

If those steps seem too much to manage, perhaps it's time you migrated to a cloud server. Since the launch of Office 365 around June 2011, Microsoft's multi-tenant server, Exchange Online, has grown year after year. According to data shared at the TEC 2020 conference, Exchange Online supports 5.5 billion mailboxes.

Migrate To the Cloud

As Silver Partners with Microsoft®, my company, Krypto IT, can migrate your business to the security of the cloud. Let a Microsoft Azure expert take over the vigilance of watching your environment. We specialize in migrating clients into the cloud. With our team of CISSPs, we can help protect your networks from hackers and have been doing so for years.

About the Author

Jerry W. Swartz, CEO Krypto IT Services – Houston, TX

Jerry W. Swartz is the founder of Krypto IT Services LLC, a Cybersecurity & IT Consulting firm based in Houston, Texas. He is an experienced Chief Executive Officer with a demonstrated history of working in the information technology, security, and service industries. Skilled in Customer Relationship Management (CRM), Data Center, Management, Software as a Service (SaaS), Outsourced Project Management and Networking Administration. Through his company, Krypto IT, he and his team of professionals provide a unique blend of scalable, remote IT & cloud-based solutions, resources, and skillsets to address today's threats and future Cybersecurity support needs of businesses & enterprises. He has been in the technology since 1995 and has been contracted by companies such as United Airlines, EDS, Memorial Hermann, and Texaco to name a few. Our clients consist of Manufacturers, Auto dealerships, Medical Practices, Law Firms, and businesses of all sizes. He is also a heart transplant survivor who goes to the local hospitals to give support and mentor patients who are waiting for transplants such as the left ventricle assist device, LVAD, recipients.

14 Ways to Protect Your Business Data

By Wade DeVore

Alan, the city's leading HVAC contractor, smiled as he walked out of the building after closing a new contract with his latest client. He knew that his specialized system that provided remote access control to his clients' buildings was his winning edge. Nothing could beat Alan's programmable controllers and he loved the fact that he could manage his clients' systems from his phone, a tablet, or his computer. Early one morning, Alan's phone began ringing off the hook; one client, then another and another reported their systems were down. Alan rushed to his computer, in shock and dismay, he saw a ransom screen. This is known as a single extortion ransom.

The calls continued: clients' building temperatures were rising, but this was only the beginning. The same connections Alan used to manage his clients' systems had also been used by the hackers to compromise Alan's business data. While his clients were calling in about their building temperatures rising, they also started seeing all of their computer systems pop up with screens demanding ransom payments. Alan's HVAC automation solution had been leveraged by the hackers to ransom all of the computers in Alan's entire client list through the small Internet of Things (IoT) devices that Alan had used to manage the HVAC systems. This is known as a double extortion ransom.

To make matters even worse, Alan's clients own list of clients started getting ransom demands. The hackers had extracted data from Alan's clients and then used that data to contact the individuals and businesses the data came from demanding ransom payments. Imagine your client list getting a ransom demand for data you maintained on them that was stolen from you? This is known as a triple extortion ransom.

Proper security is about more than antivirus and a firewall. It is about protecting your entire network from both known threats and unknown ones. It's one thing for you to be hacked. It's another thing for the hackers to get access to your clients' data, too.

Unfortunately, it wasn't over yet, not even close. Alan restored from a backup and believed that doing so prevented him from needing to pay the ransom. But the hackers had extracted all of Alan's and his clients' data before installing their ransomware. When Alan restored his backup, the hackers showed Alan proof that they had all his data. They threatened to either publish or sell it if Alan didn't pay the ransom. Alan had not encrypted his data and he ended up paying the ransom in an effort to keep the hackers from publishing or selling his data. You need more than a backup to protect yourself from ransomware; you need a skilled team and a plan.

Things have changed. According to Inc.com 60% of small and mid- sized companies go out of business within six months of a cyber attack. Data protection has become a must for all companies, regardless of size. In addition, data protection regulations around the world have added extra layers of urgency for all companies to implement curated data protection measures.

A data breach could turn into a catastrophic event for any business. The Federal Trade Commission reports there are five key principles to data security:

TAKE STOCK. Know what personal information you have in your files and on your computers.

SCALE DOWN. Keep only what you need for your business.

LOCK IT. Protect the information that you keep.

PITCH IT. Properly dispose of what you no longer need.

PLAN AHEAD. Create a plan to respond to security incidents.

Data has become the primary resource for any business or institution. There are a number of preventive steps you can take to help keep your company's data secure. The most important place to start is with a solid plan.

1. Conduct a Security Audit

You need to know which parts of your business are vulnerable. You need to know which data needs protection. You also need to know how and where that data is transmitted. It is critical that you work with a professional to audit your entire IT infrastructure. This includes all computers, networks, mobile devices, and any device attached to or that can access your network. Knowing all this will help determine what you need to do to prevent hackers from accessing your network.

2. Have a Response Plan

One of the most productive strategies your company can use to protect your business data is creating an incident response plan. Rather than having a vague idea of your policies and procedures, businesses of all sizes should have a formal IT security strategy that is as detailed as possible. It is imperative that your incident response plan not only lays out how to protect data and resources, but also cover what to do and not do should things go wrong. An incident response plan ensures you will be a step ahead. You always need to be prepared for a worst-case scenario.

It will help prevent people making rash, heat-of-the-moment decisions that might make things worse. How you respond to security incidents can be the difference between a minor data loss and a costly breach.

You should view your response plan as a critical component of your cyber security policy that will ensure your business can properly respond to a data breach. Response plans help companies adequately secure data, repair vulnerabilities, and notify the necessary individuals. It is our belief that businesses with data breach response plans are less likely to experience hacks. We believe that those with a plan in place will have less information compromised and recover faster from attacks. Faster recovery will minimize any negative impacts with your brand, data, and revenue.

Your plan should include the following initial steps:

- Disconnect the internet from your firewall and disconnect the network from any computers that have not been compromised. Powering down firewalls, switches and computer systems will lose what's in memory and will destroy evidence.
- Notify the appropriate parties. Depending on the information that was stolen, you may need to let customers and law enforcement know about it. Call your cyber liability insurance carrier and follow what they ask you to do. You do not

want to do anything that may invalidate your policy.

- Investigate what happened. Work with your cyber liability insurance carrier to investigate what went wrong.
- Do not restore over infected systems. This will destroy evidence. Restores should be to different hardware until the cyber liability insurance carrier completes their investigation.

3. Make Staff Aware of the Important Role They Play in Security and Train Them

Your staff are your front line of defense. Properly trained employees, consultants, partners, and vendors can help ensure that security breaches due to human error are minimized. One of the biggest vulnerabilities in data protection is the human factor. Executives are frequently targeted by malicious outsiders due to their level of access to data. Large companies, take special care that higher management does not circumvent the rules as it is essential that the same level of data security is maintained across the board. Provide ongoing, company-wide cyber security training, including training to recognize social engineering as well as phishing simulations.

4. Maintain Security Policies and Procedures

We must do more than just ask our employees to work securely. We must train everyone and have clear and simple policies and procedures to ensure that we are working in a secure environment. For example, require all laptops and work-from-home computers to connect to the internet through an encrypted, secured, and filtered tunnel. This protects these computers and devices from others on home and public networks. Require that no security information ever be given over the phone. Require that all authorizations to transfer large sums of money are done in person, not via email, text, or phone.

5. Keep an Information Inventory, Know Where Your Data is and Where it is Going

A critical step towards efficient data protection is knowing exactly what data is being stored and where so you can ensure it is properly encrypted and secured. Another critical step is to identify the data flow and ensure the data in motion is properly encrypted and secured. You must know where your data is at rest and in motion to make informed decisions concerning the measures needed to protect it. In the age of data protection regulations, knowing where your data is at any given moment is key, both for compliance and for building effective data protection policies.

6. Encrypt Your Data at Rest and in Motion

Encryption is a great security tool to use in case your data is stolen. If your laptop or smartphone is stolen or you lose your USB thumb drive, encryption will prevent the thieves from reading your data. The use of encryption for both data at rest (data that is currently archived) on any device and data in transit (data moving through a network, internal or external, to an endpoint destination) has become an essential step in protecting company data and securing sensitive information. Software such as data loss prevention (SLP) solutions can be added on to act as an effective method of enforcement. DLP achieves this by setting clear policies that protect and restrict access to sensitive data. Levels of access to data can be controlled based on groups and specific users or endpoints. If a user is removed in DLP from being able to access data, they will no longer be able to open the data, even if it is still in their possession.

7. Protecting Your Data in the Cloud

The first step is to choose a cloud service that encrypts your files in their cloud and on your computer. Encryption ensures that service providers and their third-party contractors do not have access to your private information. Read the user agreements with your cloud service. Those agreements explain how the service protects your information and whether you give permission for them to use or sell your information in any way by signing up. Always choose solutions that offer two-factor authentication... and use it. This means anyone who signs into your account will need extra information in addition to your password. As soon as you sign up for a cloud service provider, configure your privacy settings to ensure you are not sharing your private information.

8. Protecting Data in Your SAAS Solutions

The most important software-as-a-service (SAAS) consideration is how you protect your data. This is achieved by using various methods of data encryption both at rest and in transit. The best solutions offer you the option of controlling your encryption keys so that cloud operations cannot decrypt your data. If your SAAS provider is compromised and your data stolen, it is still secure if you are the only one that has the encryption keys. The best solutions also encrypt the data at rest. When encrypting data at rest, you gain the option of building solutions with client- side and server-side encryption for a higher level of security. You will want this flexibility in order to leverage separation of duties and audit trails. These are safeguards we must put in place to protect personally identifiable information (PII) and other critical or regulated data.

9. Maintain Encrypted Off-Site Backups

Offsite backups serve to protect us from disasters. They help us to preserve our data in the event of a system crash, disaster, or in the event of a breach. The backups should have compliant end-to-end encryption for the data in motion and compliant encryption for the data at rest. We recommend that backups be full backups that can be bare-metal restored to new hardware. We recommend discussing and planning your recovery time objective (RTO) when selecting a backup solution. Remember to regularly test restoring your backups.

10. Implement a Managed Layered Security Solution

There are many different threats working to destroy the integrity of your data; these include computer viruses, worms, and advanced hackers. They are constantly evolving and trying to find their way into your valuable data. The best defense is multiple security layers to block these threats and alert you to act appropriately against the detected threat. I wish there was an easy button to proper cyber security, but there isn't. We must constantly work to stay ahead of the bad guys.

11. Multi-Factor Authentication and Strong Passwords

Multi-factor authentication is an authentication system that requires more than one distinct authentication factor for successful authentication. This safety measure can be performed using a multi-factor authenticator or a combination of authenticators that provide different factors. The three authentication factors are: something you know, something you have, and something you are. Multi-factor authentication greatly reduces account compromise, and we highly encourage its use whenever possible. We also highly recommend strong passwords that are not reused and are kept with a secure password manager to protect your accounts.

12. Zero Trust Application Whitelisting

Zero trust application whitelisting is the gold standard when it comes to blocking ransomware, viruses, and other software-based threats. If you have not done this on an application, it is not allowed to run. Application whitelisting and ringfencing puts your business in control over what software is running on your endpoints and servers.

13. Protect Your Mobile Work Force.

You should have your own device (BYOD) policies for employee-owned devices that access company data. You should also have mobile device management (MDM) solutions to manage your mobile devices and increase protection from threats. Good BYOD policies promise to increase productivity and reduce costs. But BYOD also comes with hefty security implications. Accessing sensitive information on personal devices means that data is traveling outside the confines of the company network and puts the data at much greater risk. MDM is used to manage the devices and restrict the sort of data that can be transferred outside company devices.

MDM policies can mark a device's level of trust of a device that can be applied. Use of MDM means that employees are given the option of aligning the security of their personal devices to company policies or not. If an employee chooses not to apply, then no sensitive data is allowed on the employee-owned device.

14. Set Internal Controls to Guard Against Employee Fraud.

It is wise to use internal controls to limit your employee fraud risk, regardless of how much you trust your employees. Without proper internal controls, employees can misuse company funds or steal customer information. We recommend you limit each employee's access to only the information they need for their job. Configure your systems to log what information each employee accesses. We recommend you set up segregation of duties to prevent any single employee from having too much responsibility.

Conclusion

When it comes to proper cyber security I'd like to say there was an easy button, but there isn't. You need a skilled team to transform your technology and cyber security from a necessary evil to a tool for success. This level of expertise is not something you find just anywhere; you will need seasoned professionals that understand both your business and cyber security. You will need a team approach as well as a carefully curated best of class layered security approach.

About the Author

Wade DeVore, the CEO of NetVision Consulting, Inc. has been helping business owners manage technology challenges for twenty-six years. The NetVision team provides a curated and proven Cyber Security compliance and risk management program to assist firms in managing cyber risk. The NetVision team is headquartered in the Dallas Fort Worth Metroplex and serves clients across the United States. Wade applies the same care and attention to detail to all his clients as he does his fully restored 1950 Ford F100. Don't tinker with your technology. Call Wade DeVore and his team at NetVision Consulting for the right solution the first time.

https://www.netvisionconsulting.com

817-794-5600

Made in the USA
Las Vegas, NV
02 September 2021

29467110R00140